D0849929

HILDEGARD OF BINGEN

HEALING AND THE NATURE OF THE COSMOS

by

Heinrich Schipperges

University of Heidelberg

Translated from German
by John A. Broadwin

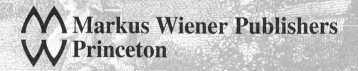
Markus Wiener Publishers
Princeton

THE TRANSLATION OF THEIS BOOK INTO ENGLISH WAS SUPPORTED
BY A GRANT FROM INTERNATIONES, BONN.

FOR INFORMATION WRITE TO: MARKUS WIENER PUBLISHERS
114 JEFFERSON ROAD, PRINCETON, NJ 08540

BOOK DESIGN BY CHERYL MIRKIN
THIS BOOK HAS BEN COMPOSED IN TIMES ROMAN BY CMF GRAPHIC DESIGN

LIBRARY OF CONGRESS CATALOGING-IN-PUBLICATION DATA
SCHIPPERGES, HEINRICH.
[HILDEGARD VON BINGEN, ENGLISH]
HILDEGARD VON BINGEN: HEALING AND THE NATURE OF THE COSMOS/
HEINRICH SCHIPPERGES
TRANSLATED FROM GERMAN BY JOHN A. BROADWIN.
INCLUDES BIBLIOGRAPHICAL REFERENCES AND INDEX.
ISBN 1-55876-137-3 HARDCOVER
ISBN 1-55876-138-1 PAPERBACK
1. HILDEGARD, SAINT, 1098–1179. I. TITLE.
BX4700.H5S2713 1996
282'.092—DC20 96-32052 [B] CIP

MARKUS WIENER PUBLISHERS BOOKS ARE PRINTED IN THE
UNITED STATES OF AMERICA ON ACID-FREE PAPER,
AND MEET THE GUIDELINES FOR PERMANENCE AND DURABILITY
OF THE COMMITTEE ON PRODUCTION GUIDELINES FOR BOOK
LONGEVITY OF THE COUNCIL ON LIBRARY RESOURCES.

Contents

ILLUSTRATIONS

I

Introduction

Often referred to yet barely known, Hildegard of Bingen is emerging as one of the greatest figures in the early history of the West—of a Europe in the ascendant—and as a still unexplored historical phenomenon that continually confronts us with new riddles.

Recall for a moment how she has been described: as a woman who founded and headed monasteries, reformed the higher and lower clergy, produced a prodigious body of written work on theology and philosophy, and left us a remarkable legacy in the fields of natural history and medicine; a woman who undertook preaching tours at an advanced age and made public appearances in marketplaces, wrote hymns and a cycle of liturgical songs together with their music; and who corresponded with notables in the empire and the Church throughout the length and breadth of Europe. Quite a woman indeed!

Even contemporaries seemed to sense Hildegard's unique qualities, acclaiming her the "Teutonic prophetess," the "jewel of Bingen," the "sibyl of the Rhine." Though much admired in her own day, she regarded herself as merely a mouthpiece, a "trumpet of God." "The throngs of the faithful," wrote Pope Eugenius III to the Abbess Hildegard around the year 1150, "burst forth in praise of you. You have become for many the perfume of life."

Hildegard's writings show us the structure of the universe as a unified whole—a universe, though, that is out of joint—and how the parts will be conjoined again for the salvation of humankind. The interrelatedness of everything—humankind and the cosmos, body and spirit, nature and grace—and the interdependence of everything were not just so many empty words to Hildegard. They went to make up a functional holistic picture of the world, down to the minutest detail. Her entire work is characterized by a clear-headed realism that focuses on the history of salvation: the vision of a world created out of nothing; the creation and fall of humanity; the Incarnation of the Son of God; and the resurrection of the body at the end of time.

In all her exegeses and catecheses, firmly grounded in dogma, Hildegard never questioned the mystery of the Godhead. She never even came close to viewing faith from a subjectivist standpoint or interpreting revelation as a stimulus to social action or as an aid to help improve people's lives. Her religious teachings contained nothing new; they simply sought to explain and proclaim traditional doctrine. Hildegard did not think or contemplate in terms of concepts. Rather, she received insights through visions, or better, by balancing one good against another and rendering a judgment based on higher authority. You will not gain access to Hildegard's world of visions, into her vision of the world, by listening to her devoutly or dissecting her with the tools of psychology. The best way to understand Hildegard is tirelessly to read her writings and contemplate her visions—visions which in turn call for written explanation and for the constant rereading of texts whose illuminations have been extolled as a true picture of the cosmos.

Hildegard's life and career unfolded during the age of Emperor Frederick I and St. Bernard of Clairvaux, during the time of the crusades and the minnesingers, in an era of dramatic political and theological upheaval. Her life spanned the reigns of seventeen popes and anti-popes, five Holy Roman emperors and German kings, and six archbishops of Mainz alone, in whose diocese her monastery at Rupertsberg was located.

The various reform movements upset and altered life in the monasteries. Crusading orders of knights came into being. The Reich (*imperium*) and the Church (*sacerdotium*) were drifting further and further apart. The long-standing Investiture Controversy was only partly resolved in the Concordat of Worms (1122), and the conflict between the empire and the papacy was coming increasingly to the fore.

The most radical changes, however, were taking place within the supposedly unassailable philosophical edifice of scholasticism. In the middle of the 12th century Aristotle's writings on natural history, along with all the scientific encyclopedias of antiquity, began to reach Western centers of education in the form of Arabic and Latin translations. Lively debates

Figure 1. Excerpt from the Ebstdorf World Atlas
from the Benedictine Ebstdorf monastery near Uelzen in the Lüneburger Heide (p. xiii)

were carried on in the schools of the High Middle Ages—Paris, Chartres, Salerno—over the Christian idea of the *imago Dei* and the Hellenistic concept of the One. The early scholastic interpretation of Genesis gave rise to a dispute over the Neoplatonic idea of emanation. Handed down with Biblical traditions, the customs of antiquity helped to form the anthropological basis of European medicine as reflected in the encyclopedias of Rabanus Maurus, Cassiodorus and Isidore of Seville.

In contrast to the philosophical currents mentioned above, Hildegard's cosmology does not confront us with the question of the validity of the cosmic order, but rather with the question of empirical knowledge of the created order and thus with the question of the knowability of the world. Humanity is the answer to the riddle of the universe, and the universe is the answer to the eternal question of humanity. "And if people do not ask the question," Hildegard wrote, "the Holy Spirit cannot provide the answer."

If you want to understand Hildegard's work in its entirety, you must do so by degrees. The singular output of this medieval woman must first be translated—on several levels: from basic yet ponderous Latin into the vernacular of modern scholarship; from the symbolism and iconography of the Middle Ages—largely unfamiliar to us—into a form of information that we can comprehend; and finally, if possible, from the visionary language that is so unmistakably characteristic of Hildegard into a picture of the world based on her visions.

Modern people, of course, no longer produce their own personal cosmologies; for reasons of methodology alone, it would be virtually impossible for them to do so. Deluged by information but still not oriented in the world, modern people seem to be caught up in a crisis. They are overwhelmed by a proliferation of idols and surrogate deities and plagued by a growing number of proselytizing sects. However, in the course of trying to find our way in this world, we sometimes stumble upon a surprisingly rich source of knowledge and inspiration. Hildegard of Bingen is just such a source!

Our study begins by putting the reader in the proper frame of mind to understand the historical upheavals taking place in the High Middle Ages and the part Hildegard played in her own time. This will help us gain a better appreciation of her life and work, at the center of which stands humanity, the peak of God's creation, destined for ultimate salvation in a transformed world.

It is clearly no accident—and seems to me of the greatest importance for humankind's situation at the turn of the millennium—that natural history and medicine occupy the central position in Hildegard's works, followed by cosmology and the history of salvation. Hildegard guides us along fantastic paths through the world of nature and the world of the spirit to the role of man in the world and as a builder of the world, i.e., to the nature of humanity, its history and destiny.

I have decided to dispense with a scholarly apparatus and supporting documentation for this study and to cite extant sources only for the most important quotations in the text. There are additional references in the complete list of primary sources as well as in the selected bibliography of secondary literature at the end of this volume.

They are only suggestions though—you'll have to read them yourself!

II

Life and Work

1. THE FORMATIVE YEARS AND ADOLESCENCE

Hildegard was born in 1098 at Bermersheim near Alzey in Rhenish Hesse, the tenth child of Hildebert and Mechthild, both of noble birth. At eight—dedicated by her parents to the Church as a "tithe" (an offering of a tenth)—Hildegard's parents placed her with Jutta von Spanheim, an anchoress at the convent of Disibodenberg near Bingen. She lived there as a recluse or *inclusa*, literally enclosed in a cell, where she was instructed in and initiated into the practices of the Benedictine movement. Benedictine monasteries were not only repositories of scholarship and the arts; they were also centers for the exchange of learning and literature. It was here more than anywhere else that we find the fruitful spiritual environment that a noble family such as Hildegard's could afford to provide for a gifted daughter.

It may be noted in passing that this esteemed Bermersheim family produced no less than seven historically documented personalities. Hildegard's brother Hugo (d. 1177) became the choirmaster of the cathedral at Mainz and was entrusted with the responsibility for training Radulf of Zähringen, the future Bishop of Liège. Another brother, Roricus, was the canon of the Benedictine abbey in the village of Tholey. Of her four sisters—Irmingard, Odilia, Jutta, and Clementia—Clementia eventually became a nun and entered Hildegard's convent.

Hildegard began her education under the tutelage of Jutta, the *magistra*. Her schooling at the convent was unusually broad and surprisingly in-depth. Yet again and again we read with some consternation her own descriptions of herself as an unlearned (*indocta*) woman—only to discover that she was in fact a remarkable individual of great erudition. Hildegard read the text of the Benedictine Rule and early learned the Psalms. She recited the Divine Office daily and read and reread the Holy

Scripture. She possessed a superior knowledge of the Old Testament and the Church Fathers and carried on a written correspondence with the leading scholars of her day. She also had the good fortune of always having a trusted assistant: the monk Volmar for many decades; the nun Richardis of Stade; and during the last years of her life the erudite Walloon monk Guibert of Gembloux. Hildegard's encounter with the learned Siward, Bishop of Uppsala may also have been an important factor contributing to the universality of her knowledge. The bishop spent some time in Disibodenberg in 1138 and dedicated three altars there. When he died in 1158 Siward left an extensive library that included an encyclopedia of plants (*Herbarium*) and a catalog of minerals (*Lapidarium*) as well as Isidore of Seville's *Etymologies* [an encyclopedia of human and divine objects] and six volumes on medicine.

At the age of sixteen the novice Hildegard took the veil from the hands of Otto, Bishop of Bamberg. When Jutta died in 1136 Hildegard was elected to head the convent at Disibodenberg. It was during these years that the young Hildegard had discovered within herself a curious intuitive gift that she called her *visio*, her ability to have visions. She saw such a great light that her soul quaked, though she was unable to communicate it to others.

Hildegard stated emphatically that she had not invented this *visio*. Nor, she said, had any other person devised or affected it. Rather, the meaning of the scriptures revealed itself to her, in visions, or more precisely, in auditory experiences, in the form of an intuitive feeling that instantly abrogated the laws of reason and produced enlightenment. Her intuition, Hildegard went on to explain, saw all things in the light of God through the five senses. The sense of sight perceived lovingly (*amat*), the sense of hearing discerned (*discernit*), the organs of taste savored (*sapit*), those of smell selected (*eligit*), and those of touch took whatever pleased them. "God, the creator of all things, is reflected in our senses." Human beings perceived God through the mirror of faith, just as the Living Light shined into the hearts of men through the same mirror. The external world was but the medium of enlightenment. "God cannot be perceived directly. Rather, he is known through creation, through humankind alone which is a mirror of all God's wonders." (CC 65: *speculum miraculorum Dei*)

In 1141, shortly after she turned forty, Hildegard had another vision, the real turning point in her career. The spirit of God touched her heart like a burning flame, transforming the silent visionary into a prophetess. The divine call became clearer and clearer. "Say and write what you see and hear!" a voice from above commanded. At first Hildegard was afraid and hesitated to act. She used illness as an escape before summoning the courage to make her visions public.

Plagued by doubts about her mission, Hildegard in 1147 turned to Bernard, the Abbot of Clairvaux, already an influential ecclesiastic, and implored him in a famous letter: "I beg you, Father, that you hear me questioning you!" Thus she began her missive, immediately addressing her concern: "I am much disturbed by a kind of vision that appears to me through the mysteries of the spirit . . . I wretched and more than wretched in the name of woman, I have looked since childhood on great wonders which my tongue could not speak about if God's spirit had not taught me to believe." Never—"not a single hour"—since her infancy had she lived in certainty. Hence her fervent plea: "So tell me what you think? I have no school knowledge about outside things. Hence my doubts and my uncertainty!" Hildegard was seeking more than consolation and solace; she hoped Bernard would give her some sign of support: "I have placed myself in your soul that you may counsel me whether you think I should tell everything publicly or remain silent!" In conclusion, she beseeched Bernard not to remain indifferent, but to answer her as someone who had a reputation as a valiant fighter: "For you uplift not only yourself, but the world, to the good of all. You are an eagle looking directly at the sun!" (Bw 26/27)

St. Bernard replied to Hildegard's letter—the first to come down to us—but he did so with great circumspection, trying diplomatically to avoid giving her an unequivocal answer. He shared Hildegard's joy that God was working through her, and he begged her to respond to the divine gift with all her heart. He admired her charisma and concluded: "What more can we teach you or how else exhort you, since you have already received instruction from within, and your anointment has enlightened you as to everything!"

St. Bernard's efforts were among the more important reasons for this humble nun becoming a *prophetissa teutonica*. At the historic synod of Trier (1147–48) he persuaded Pope Eugenius III to read aloud from

Hildegard's writings before an assembly of cardinals and priests. Prior to this the pope had sent a commission to authenticate the texts and subsequently commanded Hildegard to offer her visions to the world. The fact that Pope Eugenius had officially sanctioned some of her visions and sent her a personal letter (1152) in which he praised her "honorable reputation" and her "passion for the fire of divine love" was clearly a major turning point in Hildegard's life. She needed no other spur to finish her work.

So far as Hildegard's "visionary" experiences are concerned, they were not a case of "ecstasy" in which a soul is taken out of its body and suspended between heaven and earth. To describe her visions as a "narcissistic attempt at self-healing" (Werthmann, 1993) is as unhelpful as it is to try to portray her as an hysteric (Hattemer, 1930) or to posit the preposterous thesis that what she saw in her visions was the result of "scintillating scotomata," a form of migraine (Singer, 1917). Hildegard was clearly enthusiastic about her special faculty. However, we must not confuse enthusiasm with the kind of intoxication that impairs thinking or destroys creativity. On the contrary, the experience of the vision (the act of seeing) calls for a clear head. Filled with the divine spirit, Hildegard would begin to stir and make sounds like air passing through a "tube," a tube however through which someone else was blowing. She would then understand the world in all its richness and beauty—just as she would throughout a life-long process of maturation and, as she matured, with a growing sense of self-assurance.

Let us for a moment recall how uncertain Hildegard was in 1147 when she wrote to Bernard of Clairvaux: "I envisioned you many years ago as a man who looks directly at the sun and feels no fear, a man undaunted. I, on the other hand, cried and turned red and was timid." Having transcended her self-doubt, she was by 1175 a woman possessed of cool self-control and a superior background in all fields of knowledge, able to explain to the young monk Guibert of Gembloux humbly yet in a confident tone what it felt like to have a vision (*de modo visionis suae*): "And how is that I, poor thing, cannot know myself? God works as he will for the glory of his name and not for earthly humanity. I am always full of shaking fear, and I know not the slightest possibility of security within. And I stretch out my hand to God, so that I am sustained and carried without weight like a feather by the power of the wind." (P 332) She had seen visions, she wrote, from infancy right up to the present day, i.e., when she was over seventy!

Here is another example of the candor of her narrative and the mature nature of her confessions: "Everything I see and learn in these visions, I have long in memory; for when I see and hear this light, I remember it, and I simultaneously see, hear, know and almost in the very moment that I know, I understand. And what I do not see, I do not know, for I am une-ducated; for I have been instructed only to read with a rudimentary knowledge of the language [Latin]...Sometimes I see a light within this light, which it occurs to me to call the Living Light (*lux vivens*). And when and how I see it, I have no way of telling forth. But for the time that I see it, all sadness and all anxiety is lifted from me, and I feel like a simple young girl, and not like an old woman." (P 333)

2. THE WRITTEN WORK

During each phase of her literary career, Hildegard's output was completely original, informed with the splendid intuitive gift that makes this "cosmic poem" unique. The fact that Hildegard always had knowledgeable assistants in no way diminishes the originality of her work. The monk Volmar—"to whom she confided her secret power" (*symmysta*)—was her first secretary and advisor. Released by Abbot Kuno of Disibodenberg to assist Hildegard, Volmar served her for more than thirty years, from 1141 to 1173. Volmar was younger than Hildegard, and she mourned him after his death in 1173 as her "only beloved son." Although Volmar edited everything Hildegard dictated in order to make it conform to the rules of grammar and smoothed out any "rough" spots, he never altered the content of her accounts. The first miniature in the *Scivias* Codex depicted Volmar outside Hildegard's cell as a humble secretary in the act of transcribing a vision, while Hildegard, illuminated by the flames of the Holy Spirit, recorded her revelation directly onto a set of wax tablets.

Hildegard's second assistant was the nun Richardis of Stade, highly educated and of noble birth. Richardis was later (1151) elected abbess of the Benedictine cloister of Bassum in the diocese of Bremen, where she

Figure 2. Hildegard recording a vision in the presence of the monk
Volmar while tongues of fire from Heaven, symbolizing the experience of
divine inspiration, permeate her brain (Riesenkodex Wiesbaden,
Hessische Landesbibliothek Ms. 1 (p. XII), *Scivias*, preface)

died at a young age. Hildegard had a close personal relationship with Richardis, whom, "overflowing with love," she described as her "daughter Richardis." Together with the monk Volmar, she was depicted as Hildegard's amanuensis in a miniature in the Lucca Codex (not shown here).

Hildegard's last secretary was Guibert, a monk from the abbey of Gembloux near Namur. Guibert moved to Rupertsberg in June 1177 to act as provost for the nuns and to become Hildegard's assistant. She once beseeched the well-spoken Walloon monk: "Take no offense at the Latin of my early works, for speaking in classical phrases is not part of me, like Moses who was slow of speech and used Aaron as his spokesman and the prophet Jeremiah who was wanting in eloquence but lacked not for wisdom."

The various stages in the composition of Hildegard's literary works are best reflected in the drafts of the famous Codex 241 that was prepared between 1163 and 1174 in the scriptorium of the monastery at Rupertsberg. It was later sent to Trier and currently resides in Ghent. On the basis of these drafts it can be shown that Hildegard first recorded her visions on wax tablets. Then a scribe transferred them to parchment while correcting the grammar and adding and deleting material. Only in the third stage was a fair copy produced, i.e., a transcription of the revised text similar to those we find in contemporary manuscripts.

Anyone seeking access to the astonishing body of written work produced by Hildegard would be well advised to begin with her first theological work entitled *Scivias Domini* (*Know the Ways of God*). This seminal work, written between 1141 and 1151, consists of a series of twenty-six interconnected visions of humankind, the universe, and God in which Hildegard revealed the mysteries of the Godhead: God bathed in the divine light, the choirs of angels, the creation of humanity, the destruction of the world, the "fiery work of redemption," and the stages of salvational history—all woven together into one vast universal drama of salvation culminating in the day of judgment, when the "New Heaven and the New Earth appear."

Her second major visionary work dates from the period between 1158 and 1163 and is entitled *Liber Vitae Meritorum* (*The Book of Life's Merits*). Here too the vision proceeds from the Godhead via the cosmos directly to humankind. This work is primarily concerned with the moral decisions made by human beings during the course of their lives. These decisions are illustrated in a series of verbal battles, often graphically described, between the thirty-five virtues and vices that reflect the universal moral responsibilities of humankind.

Hildegard's vision of man and the world entitled *Liber Divinorum Operum (The Book of Divine Works)*, written between 1163 and 1173, may be regarded as her most mature and impressive achievement. In ten visions Hildegard developed her cosmological history of salvation from Genesis to the Apocalypse. Her interpretation of the opening chapter of the Gospel of St. John was the focal point of the work and presented humanity as the true center of the universe. The created order encompassed the angelic orders as well as the plants and animals. It linked the world of the senses to the life of grace and made the body and soul, the cosmos and the Church, nature and grace part of humanity's moral responsibility

Hildegard's extensive correspondence must be regarded as an integral part of her literary work, particularly since this is where she spoke most directly to us. Literally carried on across the length and breadth of Europe, it encompassed the cities of Paris, Utrecht, Stade, Halberstadt, Prague, Salzburg, Constance, Lausanne, and Clairvaux, ultimately centering on the Cologne-Trier-Salzburg area. Hildegard exchanged letters with the Holy Roman Emperor Frederick I, King Conrad II, Henry II of England and his wife Eleanor of Acquitaine, Bertha, Countess of Sulzbach and Empress of Byzantium, as well as with innumerable bishops, dukes, abbesses and abbots, priests and laypeople.

Hildegard's medical and scientific writings likewise date from the years between 1150 and 1160. They have come down to us as the *Physica (Natural History)* and the *Causae et curae (Causes and Cures)* and are ostensibly part of a single work entitled *Subtilitates diversarum naturarum creaturarum (Subtleties of the Diverse Natures of Created Things)*. In both works—especially in her discussions of physiology, pathology, and most unexpectedly in her account of the nature of sex—she spoke of a comprehensive set of correspondences between humanity and the universe, for "everything that comes under the laws of God is accountable to everything else." Everything was included in a tightly-knit system of obligations and responsibilities, correspondences and relationships.

Hildegard's unusually wide-ranging literary output had surprisingly little influence on the world of the later Middle Ages and the nascent modern era. Even scholastics during the age of Thomas Aquinas, their intellects schooled in Aristotelian logic, found it impossible to accept the spiritual assumptions that underlay her symbolist cosmology. As early as the beginning of the 13th century Gebeno, prior of the cloister at Eberbach near Rupertsberg, had collected her politically pertinent visions in his *Speculum futurorum temporum*, transforming the cosmic prophetess into a political soothsayer. Johannes Trithenius gave further respectability to this distortion of her work which was accepted even by reformers such as Andreas Osiander. Humanists, nevertheless, ridiculed the quality of its Latin, saying its language was so deficient that it could never have been inspired by the Holy Spirit.

Hildegard's remarkably wide-ranging written work is inseparable from the artistic and musical works that are a part of all her books on God and the cosmos, work and relaxation, doing and suffering. They find their loveliest expression in Hildegard's liturgical songs (*Symphoniae*), works of great artistry that magically transformed even the seeming drudgery of daily life into poetry and music. It is to this aspect of her work that we now devote our attention.

3. MUSICAL AND ARTISTIC WORKS

According to Hildegard of Bingen, human nature was fundamentally artistic and human actions were determined more by art than technology, since they were ultimately a reflection of the Creator. Hildegard referred to God himself as the master builder, a great thinker, a marvelous blacksmith. "God is like a worker (*operarius*) who blows on a fire with a pair of bellows and then turns the fire every which way so that he can accomplish his work more fully." (LVM IV, 68)

Being the superb artisan he is, God lent a helping hand to his handiwork, that is, humanity. And he would continue to work on and with humanity to the end of time. In other words, *Deus faber* created *homo faber* as his journeyman and laid down standards for humanity to follow. God in the fullness of his power (*virtus fortitudinis*) was the "supreme artisan" (*summus artifex*) and the soul his "workshop" (*fabrica summi fabricatoris*). Until the salvation of the soul, he would continue building his edifice (*aedificium et templum*) brick by living brick (PL 455 B).

Sustained by a similar spirit and disposition, Hildegard, an architect and master builder in the best sense of the word, elucidated the order that underlay the seemingly trivial activities of daily life. Beginning when she was just a young woman, Hildegard for many years studied the alterations that were regularly carried out on the monastery at Disibodenberg. It was here that she acquired a number of the ideas she later incorporated in the building of her own convent at Rupertsberg near Bingen which with its refectory, dormitories, scriptorium, and infirmary recalled the monastery at St. Gallen. Hildegard was also extremely interested in making sure that the rights of the new convent were permanently guaranteed. In 1163 she succeeded in persuading Frederick I personally to issue a letter of protection in perpetuity to ensure the free election of an abbess and the monastery's exemption from the requirement to have a secular advocate (*Vogt*) "so that the fox wouldn't break into the chicken coop." In his letter of protection Frederick threatened to exercise his "imperial rights" against anyone who dared to impose a secular advocate on the convent.

The convent at Rupertsberg was famous not only for its bold design, but also for its modern functional appointments. It had well thought-out sanitary facilities and running water in every work area. It was no accident that Matthias Grünewald (1470–1528) placed the convent at the center of his *Isenheim Altarpiece* where it appears to hover between heaven and earth.

The idea of building or constructing an edifice (*aedificare*) went to the heart of Hildegard's world of symbolism and was one of the major themes in her work. The beginning of creation and the completion of salvation appeared beneath the image of an enormous building. The Church, in particular—where the "work of redemption" was accomplished and completed—appeared in the form of a gigantic edifice. Hildegard presented the Church as the ideal place for developing spiritual strength. In her *Symphonia* she praised the Church as the City of Knowledge (*urbs scientarum*), since the entire structure was built on the humanity of Christ (*humanitas Christi principium omnis aedificationis sanctae ecclesiae*) and Mother Church would ultimately lead her children home to eternal harmony (*in supernam symphoniam*).

Figure 3. The Rupertsberg convent near Bingen in 1820
(Engraving by Eberhard Kiesern, reprinted from Daniel Meißner,
Politisches Schatzkästlein, ca. 1820)

A continuous "celestial liturgy" dominated Hildegard's artistic creations. According to her, this liturgy was sung in perfect unison (*una
voce*) and would continue forever (*sine fine*) with voices alternating (*alter
ad alterum*) in an eternal responsory. Humanity and the cosmos existed in
unique musical concord, bringing all people's hearts into consonance
(*anima symphonialis est*) and serving not only as a guide to healthy living but as the basis of an effective system of healing and therapy. All the
arts were divinely inspired, "and therefore it is only fitting that body and
soul sing hymns of praise through the voice of God." (PL 221 B)

The music Hildegard wrote for her hymns (*Symphoniae*) has been preserved in the venerable neume notation. Her melodies go beyond the
range of the Gregorian chant; the longer intervals create those poignant
effects in her compositions that cause us to listen with such rapt attention.

Musical historians regard her antiphons, sequences, responsories, and hymns as a self-contained work of art which might long ago have given rise to a "theology of music." All the arts that benefit humankind, after all, were "conceived by the same breath that breathed life into humanity." And therefore is the human soul in concord with the celestial harmonics (caelestis harmonia), and this is why the soul is tuned throughly symphonious. This was why Hildegard called her cycle of over seventy songs *Symphonia harmoniae caelestium revelationum* (*Symphony of the Harmony of Celestial Revelations*).

The human voice in song was not just an echo of paradise; it also prefigured the angelic songs of praise (*carmen angelicum*): "They bear tidings with the vibrant sound of their wondrous voices, more numerous than the grains of sand by the sea or the fruits brought forth by the earth; more varied than the sounds produced by all creatures and brighter than the glint of the sun, moon and stars on the water. Theirs is a sound more glorious than the ethereal music rising from the roaring winds that support and join together the four elements. Yet in spite of these jubilant voices even the blessed spirits are unable to comprehend the Godhead and are always devising something new to enhance their voices."

Hildegard regarded herself as a "trumpet blast of the Living Light," as a "mouthpiece." Her task was to convey messages sent by someone else. She wrote about her experiences to Elisabeth of Schönau: "Sometimes I sound like a weak trumpet of the Living Light." (Bw 197) Therefore, she said, it is also proper for us to sing "a song of rejoicing together."

Once, when Hildegard was gravely ill her fellow nuns, fearing she would die, assembled and asked anxiously: "In the event, where would we seek answers to our questions, where would we find the sounds of melodies never heard before?" According to contemporary reports, Hildegard's nuns, their hair flowing over their shoulders, stood in the choir on holidays resplendent in white silk veils, wearing golden wreaths or crowns with the sign of the cross or the image of the lamb and gold rings on their fingers—and they sang!

Apparently, Guibert of Gembloux, Hildegard's future secretary and biographer, was a frequent guest during these holiday celebrations at Rupertsberg and reported on them with enthusiasm. He noted that the abbess had a great appreciation of art and "puts words to her melodies that sing the praises of the Lord and honor the saints" and that she enhanced them "through the use of the finest musical instruments" so that they could be "sung in church." Who, Guibert exclaimed, "who has ever heard anything like this coming from a woman!"

4. THE PROPHETIC MISSION

Even while she was alive Hildegard was accorded the title "Teutonic prophetess" and acclaimed the "jewel of Bingen," the "sibyl of the Rhine." In a letter to Eckard of Dersch, Bishop of Worms (1383), Abbot Heinrich von Langenstein called her a *Theotonicorum Sibilla*. The famous Abbot Johannes Trithenius of Sponheim (1462–1516) included Hildegard in his *Catalogus illustrorum virorum Germaniae*. Even John of Salisbury (1115–1180), secretary to Theobald, Archbishop of Canterbury, was enthusiastic about Hildegard's prophetic writings and wrote to his friend Girardus la Pucelle: "Send me whatever visions and prophecies of the blessed and most renowned Hildegard you have in your possession. I consider her to be most commendable and admirable, for our Pope [Eugenius III] has embraced her with his warm love and friendship."

While having complete faith in her prophetic powers [in the prophetic mode of annunciation], Hildegard clearly dissociated her prophecies from more popular forms of predicting the future. Although the many wonders of God were given to her in visions, the "future fate of humankind" was not revealed to her. "I do not presume to investigate the future of created beings, because it is better for the soul not to know [the future]." She regarded it as her prophetic mission not to satisfy human curiosity, but to convey the "depth of the Holy Scriptures" granted to her in visions (Sc I, 3). Hildegard had to work out the visions in her own mind before the "mysterious quaking" of this "very ordinary woman" (*simplex homo*) evolved into the audacious prophetic language that was made known to emperors and kings, popes and prelates. The mystical vision had become gospel, the visionary insight public pronouncement.

Hildegard clearly regarded herself as a prophetess and did not shrink from comparing herself to the great prophets of the Old Testament, Isaiah and Ezekiel, whose mode of prophesying—obviously with reference to her own experience—she described as follows: "They also had a certain hardness like the solidity of marble (*marmorea soliditas*), because having been filled with the Holy Spirit, they did not cringe before anyone but always stood firm with the integrity of truth (*in integritate veritatis*). They did not cut their words, since they accepted what they said from no one other than the one who is complete integrity, namely, God (*totus integer Deus*). They were as inflexible as stones and did not give ground to anyone else. They acted in the whiteness of simplicity, in the simplicity of an infant that does not speak other than what it sees and knows." (LVM II, 38)

Hildegard's meeting with Frederick I and the exciting exchange of letters that ensued is a perfect example of her prophetic manner. The conversation between the abbess and the emperor took place in the Palatinate near Ingelheim in the year 1150. Frederick confirmed the fact that the encounter actually took place and that Hildegard made a prophecy during their meeting. The emperor promised Hildegard: "We shall never cease making every effort in behalf of the empire's honor."

Hildegard, however, was skeptical and beseeched the emperor to remain a "well-armed warrior." In a letter (1164) written after the schism that resulted from Frederick's confirmation of Paschal III as "anti-pope," Hildegard became more explicit, warning: "Be wary lest the highest King strike you to earth for the blindness of your own eyes which do not see aright, how you should hold that scepter in your hand for right ruling!" Since Frederick refused to change his policy toward the papacy—in 1168 he "elected" Calixtus III anti-pope in opposition to the incumbent Alexander III—Hildegard sent another letter to the emperor, this time an angry missive, and condemned him for his "obduracy." "Hear this," she concluded, "if you wish to live! Or I run you through with my sword!" Hildegard never received a reply, but she did live to see Frederick and Pope Alexander III make peace in Venice in April 1177.

The holistic nature of her cosmology helps explain her vigorous criticism—so unusual at the time—of the age in which she lived, an age which she called "womanish" or "effeminate" (*tempus muliebre*). In a letter to Pope Anastasius IV she also called it a "modern" age, where money alone ruled the world by means of a diabolical tyranny, where charlatans ostensibly cried out for peace but were arming for war, where the world delighted in empty diversions and even the sacred city of Rome was moribund. "For the eye rages, the nose robs, the mouth kills." (Bw 39/40) In sum, this was a womanish age which Hildegard not only polemicized against but actively challenged. She spoke in convents and in the marketplaces of major cities to demand publicly a reform of the clergy and to preach against the Cathari.

Her first sermons on ecclesiastical politics, still timely today, were directed against the Cathari. In the middle of the 12th century the Cathari, whose name means "the pure," were propagating their faith chiefly in the Rhineland. They claimed to be "filled with the Holy Spirit." But according to Hildegard they "would catch themselves a woman only to indulge in lustful pleasures." The Cathari came from the East in the company of merchants and crusading knights, settling in Cologne around 1140 and quickly spreading across France to northern Italy. They sought to combine the ideas of the poverty movement with the dualistic beliefs of the neo-Manichaeans, that is, that God had created the pure soul alone; whereas, Satan had created the material body. A Cathar council (1167) split the sect into Waldensians who called for evangelical poverty and Albigensians who organized a counter-church.

It was not only the Cathari's extreme asceticism—their rejection of marriage, the priesthood and the eucharist—that Hildegard challenged, but, even more so, the gnostic ideas that underlay the beliefs of these sectarians who held the body in contempt and renounced sexuality. Hildegard put forward her own ideas in opposition, i.e., that humanity's relationship to God and the universe was inseparable and that for her there existed only *one* reality. She insisted that humanity was incontrovertibly material creation and spirit and at the end of the world would be transformed in soul and body and live on "serenely and in perfect harmony."

The spiritual crisis that was besetting ever greater numbers of people was reason enough for the abbess of Rupertsberg to set out from her convent—in her sixties no less—and undertake a series of arduous journeys. Of her major preaching tours, detailed descriptions of four have come down to us. Hildegard's first tour in 1160 took her to Mainz, Würzburg, Ebrach, and Bamberg, her second to Lorraine by way of Trier and Metz. A few years later (1161–1163) we find her traveling to Siegburg and Cologne via Boppard and Andernach and thence to the Ruhr. Around

1170 the aged abbess set off on her final preaching tour, to Maulbronn, Hirsau, and Zwiefalten. The tours were exhausting undertakings, and Hildegard would travel variously on horseback, in a boat, in a carriage or on foot. Documents attest to the fact that she covered an average of twenty-five to thirty kilometers per day.

Even now it is worth rereading the sermons that Hildegard put into writing at the behest of various clerics, such as the sermon she preached at Cologne: "You are the night exhaling darkness, an unbending lot who do not even walk in the light because of your affluence . . . You look only at your own works. You do or abandon at your own pleasure." And further: "You do not have eyes, since your works do not shine before men with the fire of the Holy Spirit, and you do not meditate upon good examples for them. For just as the winds blow and penetrate the whole world, so should you be mighty winds teaching all people. But you are worn out by seeking after your own transitory reputation in the world, so that, at one moment, you are knights, the next slaves, the next mere jesting minstrels, so that in the perfunctory performance of your duties you sometimes manage to brush off the flies in the summer."

They ought to be the day, spiritual leaders, Hildegard wrote of the clerics of Cologne, but instead they were the night, the darkness, in which they lay as if already dead. They were so worn out by pursuing the transitory glories of this world that the best they could manage was the perfunctory performance of their duties. "You should be the strong corners of the Church, holding it up, like the corners that hold up the ends of the earth. But you do not hold up the Church. Because of your disgusting riches and avarice, you do not properly teach your subordinates, saying foolishly, We can't do everything! And so they are scattered and do whatever they wish. You ought to be a pillar of fire and embrace discipline. But you are deceiving yourselves when you say, We have no control over any of them! And because you are not doing this, you are mocked with the words of the Psalms: 'They reel and stagger like drunkards, and all their wisdom is swallowed up.'" (PL 244 A–253 B)

Never before had a woman spoken out so boldly, so outrageously. She utterly confounded her contemporaries. With Hildegard's prophetic voice ringing in our mind's ear, we can begin to understand her mystical mission—one that differed radically from the vocation of those 13th and 14th century "women mystics engulfed by love of God" whose language paralleled that of the minnesingers and who remind us of the later prophets of the Old Testament who were less concerned with making predictions than issuing warnings and calling for divine judgment.

What lifts Hildegard above the mysticism of the waning Middle Ages and the Gothic set of doctrines known as scholasticism is the fact that by her prophetic mode of living she set an example for a strife-torn age. Combining vision and reality, symbolism and philosophy, she stands like the figure of Dante at the center of Western Christian traditions that are still largely to be explored.

5. The Final Years

Hildegard's entire life, wrote the chronicler, was one splendid vision of dying, particularly during her final years when she was increasingly afflicted with various physical ailments and subject to the sudden pressures of outside challenges. Yet what the outer shell lost in terms of physical power, according to the *Vita*, "the inner self recouped through the spirit of science and strength. And as the body wasted away, the wondrous fire of the spirit burned inside her with greater brightness." (V I, 2) In the spirit of Benedictinism Hildegard lived every hour of her daily life with a keen eye to maintaining discipline: "She never left her chosen *vita activa* to return to mere trivial pursuits; instead, she found relaxation in mystical contemplation, at the other end of the scale of human activity. God, however, did allow her to return from the contemplation of His inexhaustible majesty to the burdens of her *vita activa*. Thus she was active in the flesh and at the same yearned for the divine light in spiritual contemplation." (V I, 9)

Further on in the chronicle we read that throngs of people—women as well as men—poured into Rupertsberg to seek counsel regarding their personal problems. The sick received advice and remedies for what ailed them. Even Jewish scholars came to debate with Hildegard, "and she refuted them using their own arguments." When she spoke "about the nature of humanity, the struggle between the spirit and the flesh or gave the example of the Holy Father," she always displayed "common sense." Severely disabled by illness herself, Hildegard, as she wrote to Guibert, felt "mired in pains so great they threaten to kill me. So far, though, God has always revived me."

The last year of Hildegard's life was clouded by one of the gravest and bitterest crises she ever had to face. The clergy of Mainz issued an interdict against her monastery at Rupertsberg forbidding the celebration of the mass and greatly angering the aged abbess, particularly since she had been forbidden to recite her beloved *canticum laudum* (canticle in praise of God).

How did the conflict arise? Hildegard had permitted the burial of a certain excommunicated nobleman in the cemetery of her monastery. The dead nobleman had supposedly been reconciled to the Church at the time of his death and been absolved from the interdict. When the prelates of Mainz found out what had happened, they ordered Hildegard to have the corpse exhumed and removed, otherwise they would impose an interdict on the monastery. What did Hildegard do? She refused to cast out from holy ground a man who had been granted absolution and had received the eucharist. She went to the man's tomb with her *baculus* and erased all traces of the grave.

In an impromptu letter of protest to the prelates of Mainz (PL 218–243), Hildegard implored the clerics not to cut her off from an essential part of her life, i.e., from singing praises to God. She explained in moving words the divine origin of the canticle and propounded, as it were, a theory of music: "While he was still innocent, before his transgression, Adam's voice blended fully with the voices of the angels in their praise of God." In accord with their spiritual nature, the angels were grouped in choirs. Adam lost his angelic voice because of his sin. But God wished to restore in Adam the light [of truth], the pristine memory of creation that he possessed before the fall.

With respect to Adam's restoration, the prophets not only composed psalms and canticles, but constructed various kinds of musical instruments as well, the purpose of everything being to admonish and arouse (*admoniti et exercitati*) their listeners and edify them with regard to internal things. Meanwhile, the devil never ceased trying through wicked suggestions and distractions to eradicate the sweet beauty of spiritual hymns (*pulchritudinem divinae laudationis et spiritualium hymnorum*) from human hearts, causing discord throughout the community.

Hildegard went on to argue forcefully that the prelates should beware lest "Satan, who drove man from celestial harmony and the delights of paradise" (*a caelesti harmonia et a deliciis paradisi*) circumvent them. The decision to forbid the singing of praise to God (*canticum laudum*) must not be taken lightly. For just as Jesus Christ was born of the Virgin Mary through the Holy Spirit, so, too, the canticle of praise was rooted in the Church through the Holy Spirit, "reflecting celestial harmony" (*secundum caelestem harmoniam*). Therefore we must praise God with clashing cymbals. It was no accident that people sighed and groaned at the sound of singing, for they recalled the nature of the celestial harmonies (*symphonialis est anima*). Hildegard concluded by warning the clerics not to continue their prohibition of the singing of God's praises. Those who impose silence on a Church "will lose their place among the angelic choirs" (*carmen angelicum*).

In the spirit of early medieval musical theory, familiar to us from Boethius's *De Musica*, Hildegard believed in the idea of "cosmic harmony" (*musica mundana*) and described how each of the elements possessed a characteristic "pristine sound that it had at the time of creation" and how the melodies of celestial harmony (*harmonia elementorum*) were combined in a "symphony of harps and zithers." (PL 1049 C) This was the reason she praised the elements so highly: "Fire has flames and sings in praise of God. Wind whistles a hymn to God as it fans the flames. And the human voice consists of words to sing paeans of praise. All creation is a single hymn in praise of God." (P 352)

There then appeared the figure of humanity (*musica humana*), of harmonious proportions and in concord with the celestial harmonies (*musica mundana*). The human soul also had harmony (*symphonia*) in itself, and the human heart was like a symphony (*symphonizans*); it was perfectly conjoined, rooted in the pristine sounds of paradise, and it aspired to harmony (LVM IV, 59). The soul of humanity was but a melody composed of the beautifully arranged sounds of paradisical innocence.

It was as a reflection of this exalted harmony that we experienced the possibilities inherent in instrumental music (*musica naturalis*), which Hildegard described in terms of her laws of numbers and sound, melody and rhythm—instrumental music that led directly to the artistic achievements in music with which we are familiar today (*musica instrumentalis*).

The musical instruments she mentioned most often were zithers and flutes, horns and trumpets, drums and cymbals, and time and again the organ.

As the dispute over the interdict became increasingly bitter and escalated as a result of various interventions, an apparently irreconcilable conflict erupted between the clergy as an institution and Hildegard as a charismatic personality. The prelates at Mainz adhered stubbornly to the letter of the law; whereas Hildegard followed the dictates of her heart. The case was finally settled through the personal intercession of Christian, Archbishop of Mainz, and the interdict was lifted in 1179. However, the affair seems to have sapped the aged abbess's mental and physical strength.

The chronicler spoke emotionally of Hildegard's final years: "After the holy mother had with dedication successfully fought many an arduous battle, she wearied of life and daily wished for release to be with Christ." (V IIII, 27) Hildegard died on 17 September 1179 in her monastery at Rupertsberg. The author of the *Vita* (V III, 27) wrote of a wondrous light that appeared over her deathbed in the form of a cross and felt that by giving this sign God wished to indicate "with how much light he celebrated the arrival of his beloved servant in the Kingdom of Heaven."

When Hildegard was dying at Rupertsberg, she was already a prophetess and wished for nothing more than to open people's hearts and minds to reality, to a world in which humanity, as God's creature, would in turn become the builder of a complete universe. With her view of the world and her world of symbols, Hildegard represents a unique phenomenon in Western intellectual history, a woman as scintillating as she was sensitive, a "fragile vessel of a woman" (*paupercula feminea forma*), a woman in whom again and again a "woman's verdant zest for life" came into full flower.

We can now understand why even in her own day Abbot Rupert of Königstal could exclaim with enthusiasm: "The sharp-witted professors in the kingdom of the Franks could never have accomplished anything similar. With their desiccated hearts (*arenti corde*) and puffy cheeks (*buccis afflatis*) the most they can do is make a dialectical fuss and get bollixed up in rhetorical hairsplitting. This godly woman, on the other hand, lays stress on one thing only, that which is necessary. She draws from the wellspring of her inner resources and pours out her treasures." (P 384)

We would be well advised, wrote her biographer Guibert of Gembloux, to drink deeply of Hildegard's spring, for we do not want "to be like the ass that carried wine but never sampled it."

III

The World and
Humanity

1. The Spiritual Setting

Leaving aside all naturalistic interpretations, we have to interpret Hildegard's vision of humanity and the cosmos in terms of its spiritual setting alone. And the spiritual structure of her universe comes alive only when we view it in terms of the mystery of the triune Godhead. Her first vision, "On the Construction of the Universe," began with a mystical image which Hildegard described as follows:

"I saw within the mystery of God, amid the southern winds, a beautiful image. It had a human form. Its countenance was of such beauty and radiance that I could have more easily looked at the sun than at that face. A wide golden ring encircled its head. In this ring above the head another face appeared, like that of an elderly man. Its chin and beard rested on top of the first head. On either side of the figure a wing grew out of its shoulder." (LDO I, 1)

Then, as characteristically happened with Hildegard, the vision became audible and the figure began to speak: "I, the fiery life of divine essence, aflame beyond the beauty of the fields, I glisten in the waters and burn in the sun and moon and stars. With every breeze I awaken everything to life. The air lives by turning green and being in bloom. The waters flow as if they were alive. The blazing sun lives in its light, and the moon is enkindled by the light of the sun and brought to life again and again . . . For I am life, whole and entire (*integra vita*)—not struck from stones, not blooming out of twigs, not rooted in a man's power to beget children. Rather all life has its roots in me. Reason is the root, the resounding Word blooms out of it." (LDO I, 2)

This was the basic trinitarian structure of being, pictured in ever new and often quite startling images. Three qualities distinguished reason (*rationalitas*)—sound, words, and breath. In the Father was the Son, as

Figure 4. A youthful figure representing love, under the paternal
figure of kindness, carries a lamb to symbolize gentleness
(Cod. lat. 1942, Folio 1^V, page xiii, Bibliotheca Governativa di Lucca)

words were in sound. The spirit was in both, as were breath and words. And the spirit of the Lord filled the earth and manifested itself in the beauty of nature. Earth's greening power (*viriditas*) caused the buds to bloom and the blossoms to produce fruit. The clouds drifted along their paths. The moon and the stars blazed with fiery power. Dry wood caused fresh blossoms to sprout from the greenery. Water welled up as lightly as a breeze and poured down in torrents.

Everything on earth inhaled and exhaled in an atmosphere of wetness and moisture: "There are three qualities in a stone and three in flame and three in a word. In the stone is damp greenness, solidity to the touch, and sparkling fire . . . Similarly, as the flame with its incandescence has three qualities, so there is one God in three persons. The flame burns with brilliant light and purplish fire and fiery heat . . . And as three causes are active in producing words, so the Trinity in the Unity of the Divinity may be deduced. How? A word is composed of sound, power and breath. It has sound that it may be heard, power that it may be understood, and breath that it may be pronounced." (Sc II, 2)

Similarly, sex had three qualities that Hildegard compared, in a bold analogy, to the interrelationship of the three persons in the Godhead. Sexual potency (*fortitudo*) was symbolized by the Father and the libido (*concupiscentia*) by the loving Son, who was manifested in the Holy Spirit (*studium*). Sex was a reflection, a mirror image of the Godhead (Sc II, 3). In a similar manner, we only became truly human and capable of comprehending God's work and the reality of the spirit through physical union with another human being.

Hildegard constantly devised new images to illustrate the life of the Trinity, its vital power and compassionate wisdom. "God is he who lives and who is capable and who knows. In him all his works have the potential of perfection. All his works have become distinct and made perfect with these three powers. God is eternal, and fire is eternal, and God is here. He is not a hidden fire nor a silent flame, but an effective fire. God is beyond the mind and understanding of all creatures. In the clarity of his mysteries and secrets he dispenses over everything and rules over everything, just as the head rules over the whole body. For God makes life rational when eyes see, ears hear and noses smell; and he speaks reasonable words." (LVM I, 36/37)

Figure 5. The Trinity in the Unity (Riesenkodex Wiesbaden, Hessische
Landesbibliothek Ms 1 (p. XII), *Scivias* II, 2)

The existence of the Trinity kept the universe in motion and gave rise to the spiritual encounters that continually took place in the angelic choirs. And the angels "behold at the very fountainhead of life the beating of the eternal heart." It was at this same source that humanity also beheld with its own eyes "the intense energy emitted by the heart of the Father." (P 445)

Using similarly vivid imagery Hildegard elucidated the spiritual setting of the created order. Beyond the universe there appeared the triune Godhead whose essence was reason guided by divine love. Humankind gained sustenance for its life and culture from the power of the trinity; man was stamped, as it were, with the trinitarian seal. When God created the world, he created the human being in his own image and likeness, marking it with the sign of both his higher and lower creatures. God so loved humanity that he offered it the position once occupied by his fallen angel along with the honor and glory that the bad angel had lost as a result of rebelling against Heaven.

Hildegard went a step further, for she regarded the incarnation of the Son of God as indisputably predestined: "When God created the world, he decided in his eternal wisdom that he would become human" (CC 50: *homo fieri voluit*). By accepting this doctrine Hildegard, like Rupert of Deutz and later Duns Scotus, had clearly espoused the *praedestinatio Christi absoluta*; whereas St. Bonaventura and Thomas Aquinas viewed the Incarnation as a consequence of the first sin, a fact that had far-reaching implications for Western Christian philosophy.

It was no accident that the cosmic disk or wheel was located not just in the Godhead's chest, but in its very heart (*in pectore*). The living wheel (*rota*) was, as it were, an organ of the Godhead, it was the heart of God (*operatio Dei*). As the cosmic wheel turned, it stood not only for the idea of order in the universe, but for an evolving world as well. The wheel symbolized the working of nature (*opus cum creatura*) and the forces of history, the interplay of the seasons and the periods of life, and the tragedy inherent in the vicissitudes of change (*vicissitudo temporum*).

Nowhere—at least upon a cursory examination—was Hildegard's theological worldview dogmatic or moralistic. Rather, it was artistic and erotic in nature, sustained by a spiritual mysticism. Her message of salvation was supported by a pedagogical principle and motivated by the desire to provide therapy. The message of Hildegard's first vision of mankind and the world was that humanity was in the process of being healed and saved.

With these visions fresh in her mind and after pondering the turning of the cosmic wheel, Hildegard stepped back in amazement and exclaimed: "O human being, look to humanity. For humanity has the heavens and earth and all created things within itself. It is one form (*forma una*) within which all things are hidden." (CC 2) The celestial harmonies were a mirror of the divinity, and human beings were a mirror of all God's wondrous works!

2. HUMANITY IN THE COSMOS

Hildegard's *Book of Divine Works*, her speculations on humankind and the cosmos, might best be compared to a house in which one can clearly discern the various stages in its construction and the types of material used. At the heart of the structure, at its very center, stood the awesome vision of the Incarnation of the Word of God. In the beginning was the Word and it was made flesh. The core of the vision was the belief that the Word in person had entered the life of humanity, that the Logos had become human. Two "wings," as it were, adjoined the cosmic "house"— the six days of creation as chronicled in the Book of Genesis and the visions described in St. John's Gospel. God's Word linked the cosmos to the history of salvation.

The fact that Hildegard's cosmology is neither a mystical transformation of the world nor the result of an ecstatic visionary experience becomes immediately clear when Hildegard projects her vision of the cosmos in concrete terms, that is, in terms of humankind which occupied the supreme place in the cosmos: "For humankind is more important than all other creatures that remain dependent on the world. Although small in stature, humanity is powerful in soul. Humanity's head is turned upward and its feet to the solid ground, and it can place into motion both the higher and the lower things." Humanity was not merely suspended in the cosmic net but had the cosmos firmly in its grip and was like a person who holds a net in hand and shakes it. God fortified the human species with the powers of nature: "God has buckled upon people the armor of creation so that they can know the whole world through sight, understand it through hearing, distinguish it through smell, be nourished by it through taste, and dominate it through touch."

Thus the human being exists as a unitary work (*unum opus*): "We understand this unitary *opus* when we see how the soul brings air to its bodily organism through its thought processes. It brings warmth through every power of concentration; it brings fire through the intake of matter; in addition, it brings water by incorporating water materials and greening power (*viriditas*) through the process of procreation. And we humans are put together in this way at the first moment of creation. Up above and down below, on the outside as well as on the inside, and everywhere—we exist as corporeal beings. And this is our essence." (LDO IV, 103) This is the human being (*et sic est homo*)!

To Hildegard the universe was synonymous with humanity. By adhering to her anthropological worldview she was able to strike a balance between those who ventured into biologistic utopias and those who indulged in the excesses of spiritualism. She eschewed Christian gnosticism and the idealist contortions of Western philosophy. It was always the real world of humankind that came to the fore in her vision entitled "On the Construction of the World" (*De operatione Dei*).

Being God's privileged creature (*opus operationis Dei*), humanity was endowed with excellent faculties and stood at the pinnacle of visible creation. As a builder (*homo operans*) humankind's mission was to be an expressive reproduction of the creator's infinite perfection. As a reflection of the cosmos (*speculum universi*) humanity was destined to bring its potentialities to reality. And as a rational being (*homo rationalis*) humankind engaged in an ongoing dialogue with the cosmos and was responsible for the salvation of the whole world (*homo responsurus*).

THE COSMOS IN RELATION TO HUMANITY

In a powerful illumination from the *Book of Divine Works* a human figure is shown standing directly in front of the earth, which is ocher in color and appears at the center of the cosmos. The earth is encircled by a broad band of luminous air (*aer lucidus*). Deep-hanging clouds descend from the bluish upper quadrants with rain pouring out of them in streams. A thin stratum of air (*aer tenuis*) is enclosed in a more powerful band (*aer fortis*) which is in turn surrounded by a wide circle of watery air (*aer aquosus*) represented by wavy lines. Above this is a star-spangled band of pure ether (*purus aether*) framed by a wreath of flaming red leaves. Strange-looking animals at the top portion of the ether exhale their powerful breath toward the interior of the cosmic wheel, at the center of which stands the human figure (LDO II, 1).

All the elements of the universe, together with the winds, stars and planets, constitute the "firmament" or world fortress, i.e., the outermost shell or circle of the world. The firmament is strengthened by fire, kept in motion by the ambient air, moistened by the watery air, illuminated by the stars, and sustained by the power of the winds. All the spheres are bound to each other and to the world. None can exist without the other. Each is curbed by the whole. The universe is an orderly cosmic unity. In the midst of the cosmos appears a human figure standing upright, arms extended. Its head is projected upward; its feet rest on firm ground. Its hands are outstretched to the right and the left to enclose the disk of the universe. For just as the human body exceeds the heart in size, so also are the powers of the soul more powerful than those of the body (LDO II, 15).

God made humanity from the same material with which he created the cosmos. He endowed the human being with the spirit of reason so that the world would be at its command and he could collaborate with humankind on the evolution of the universe. God's plan (*praescientia Dei*) for human beings was that, being the center of creation, they could help him in realizing the potentialities of the world (*opus cum creatura*). It was God alone, however, who reinforced the cosmos by creating the winds and who illuminated it by making the stars, and it was he who consolidated the status of the earth by placing it at the center of the firmament, for he himself wished to take from earthly matter the garment of flesh for the incarnation of his son (*terra materials opus Dei est, qui materia humana filii Dei est*).

We have drawn a bead on the fundamental elements that make up humanity's place in the cosmos: the human being as a creature dependent upon God (*opus Dei*); humanity working together with God (*opus alterum per alterum*), and humankind's responsibility in and to the world (*opus cum*

Figure 6. Humanity at the center of the universe
(Cod. lat 1942, Biblioteca Governativa Lucca, p. XIII)

creatura). Let us now briefly review these obligations. First and foremost, the human being is the handiwork of God (*opus Dei*). It is simply impossible to conceive of humans as purely autonomous beings. Humankind simply cannot be the result of evolution or the by-product of chance. Humans are, rather, created beings; they are and continue to be eminently material creatures, and their bodies are therefore subject to the ravages of time. Human beings are obedient, yet also rebellious; they are fragile and in need. In their personal relationships they always devote themselves to another, and their devotion is always validated in terms of another.

Second, humans could not exist in isolation, without reference to anyone else or as ends in themselves, as abstract beings. Rather, God purposely designed them as male and female to live in a reciprocal relationship (*opus alterum per alterum*) in which one human being realized itself through and together with another and then set itself in motion. However, we would not learn the purpose of self-realization until we saw the big picture and understood the world.

Third and last, humanity does not exist for its own sake, to find or realize itself. People have a task to perform in the outside world, namely, to work with and upon nature (*opus cum creatura*). They have, as it were, an ecological responsibility. Thus every creature is linked to another, and every essence was constrained by another (*creatura per creaturam continetur*).

Just as the rising sun sent forth its beams, God caused all his creatures to rise at the beginning of the world. He not only led them to the light; he caused them to develop, with ever greater awareness, their own "fullness of fertility." To understand humanity as a totality, we had to understand not only the external world, but its history as well, that is, the entire history of salvation.

Hildegard's image of humanity was permeated, as it were, by all the natural forces of the cosmos. Hence the joy that people derived from their existence and their sensual make-up (*constitutio*), hence their existential sympathy for all the suffering in the world (*destitutio*), and therefore also the struggle of all creatures to restore themselves (*restitutio*). Throughout the world the Spirit truly turned everything green and ripened into fruit; in the light of nature life truly became reality.

The nature of human beings was explicable only on the basis of their connection to the cosmos. Just as the Son of God dwelled in the heart of the Father, so humanity stood at the center of the world (LDO IX, 9). The cosmic order in which man was the symbol of the whole world derived from the essential interdependence of Creator and creature (*omnis creatura*) (LDO II, 32). This was the reason that humanity appeared as a being brimming with life (*vita est*) and exuded an aura of vitality (LDO IV, 105).

Anyone who put their trust in God the Creator would necessarily have to revere the enduring existence of this terrestrial world—the orbits of the sun and the moon, the wind and the air, fire, earth and water, i.e., everything God had created to honor and protect humanity. Humankind had no other reality and no other source of stability. If they forsook these guideposts as they oriented themselves in the world, they would, according to Hildegard, have no knowledge of themselves or the world. They would deprive themselves of the protection of the angels and be destroyed by demons (LDO II, 22).

In this sense, the human species was by its very nature *opus*, a vigorous and responsible work of God; whereas the nature of the angels was *laus*, the worship of God through hymns of praise, and the work of the rest of creation was *sonus*, i.e., the mute whisperings of the natural world, the roar of water as it surged and plunged into abysses. Thus humans incorporated the whole world within their physical being by actualizing all things in the flesh.

3. The Nature of the Body

In the very first vision of her magisterial holistic cosmology, Hildegard asserted with prophetic certainty that the universe created by God would come into full bloom only as humanity itself evolved and only as a result of human effort (*opus per hominem floreat*). At the apex of her cosmology—the powerful vision of the Incarnation—Hildegard revealed the name of that flower. It was neither the spirit nor the soul, but rather the body human, the omnipresent manifestation of human existence (*corpus ubique*). On the outside as well as on the inside, up above and down below (*extra et intra, supra et subtus*), the human being was nothing other than a body.

The body, that universal medium, was in fact the world. What this meant in terms of Hildegard's work can be illustrated with an example. It was our stomachs—not our brains or hearts—that God had endowed with the capacity to "comprehend" the cosmos (*capax mundi*). By the same token, the cosmos was nothing more than a giant stomach passing cosmic matter through us while we lived on earth (*capacitatem mundi ostendit*). Hence our stomach always craved the strength of the creatures it took in and then passed on, both to sustain itself and to establish the correspondence of microcosm and macrocosm.

This is but one of many examples of the way in which Hildegard viewed humanity, that is, always in holistic and concrete terms, often naively but always as a quintessentially physical creature, which was the only way in which we could understand its inner essence. This is why she discussed the stomach and the other parts of the body—from head to toe—in such great detail and why she linked her discussion to the prologue of the Gospel of St. John in order to demonstrate in concrete terms how the Word became flesh, how limb by limb it was made flesh in our world, for all people and all time.

We are thus getting closer to the idea of the body as Hildegard first sought to understand it in its pristine, purely physiological manifestation in paradise, which she described as its "primal state" (*constitutio prima*) or as the place of its "mystical genesis" (*genitura mystica*).

At the beginning of her medical work entitled *Causae et curae* Hildegard described the primitive state of humanity in simple but poignant terms: "The elements in the world are also in human beings, and people work with them. They are fire, air, water, and earth. These four elements are so closely interconnected that one cannot be completely separated from the other. They maintain themselves so tightly together that people call them the 'firmament,' the fixed foundation of the cosmos." (CC 3)

Again using the simplest of terms, Hildegard described not only how the elements combined to form the cosmos, but also how they helped to shape and give life to our own puny human bodies: "When God made humanity, the earth out of which it was formed (*limus*) was glued together by water. God sent the breath of life—fire and air—into this form made from earth and water. Because the human form was made from earth and water, the earth became flesh through the fire of this breath of life and through the air, the water, through which the earth was held together, became blood. When God made Adam, His radiance instantly embraced the entire earth out of which Adam was made. This earth showed itself outwardly in Adam's fashioning—in the shape of his limbs—but Adam was hollow within." (CC 42)

Hildegard went on to describe how in similar fashion the inside of the body was formed—the heart, liver, stomach, bowels, brain, and the other inner organs. The soul was fiery like air and moist, and it filled the entire human heart which pumped the elemental forces throughout the body. The liver heated the heart, the lungs covered it, and the stomach was a place (*habitaculum*) within the human body for the reception of food. The heart was the seat of all knowledge, the liver was the seat of the emotions. The lungs were like veins in the leaf of understanding (*rationalitas*). The mouth was a mouthpiece and brought forth the voice. The ears were like two wings that guided all the tones in and out. The eyes were paths for mankind, the nose transmitted taste (*sapientia*)—and so on and so forth for all the body's other organs (CC 42/43).

People were made from the four elements—earth, air, fire and water—and these constituted their inner existence. From fire they derived their warmth, from the air their breath, from water their blood and from the earth their flesh. Or to put it another way: "Human beings derive their power to see from fire, from air their hearing, from water their movement, and from the earth their pace. The earth prospers when the elements fulfill their duties in a good and orderly fashion so that the heat, the dew, and the rain divide and come down moderately at the right time to give the earth and the fruits the best weather conditions and bring forth much fruit and health." (CC 49/50)

Thus God created both the cosmos and the human being—the microcosm—out of the four elements. "As the elements hold the world together, so they are responsible for the well-being (*compago*) of the human body. They are spread through (*effusio*) the body and divide their tasks (*officia*) so that the human being can exist in a solidly built and perfectly balanced organism, in the same way that the elements are regarded as the substance and workspace of the natural world." (CC 49)

Figure 7. Human passage through life: The soul enters its tent, the human body (Cod. lat. Ms. 1 (ca. 1165), Hessische Landesbibliothek Wiesbaden, *Scivias* I, 4)

The macrocosmic scheme of the human body—with its cranium, chest, and limbs—corresponded to the forces of the universe and paralleled the world of the senses and the life of grace. The human feet corresponded to the rivers and carried people throughout their lives on earth. The human nose corresponded to the sphere of air and symbolized the natural order and culture. It was also the organ of wisdom and discrimination and helped man orient himself in the world and view it dispassionately. On the other hand, the cosmos, as we indicated above, was depicted as a giant stomach. The cosmos and the stomach were storage places for cosmic matter and exemplified human beings' existential connection to the universe, which was in turn reflected in their moral life through the ongoing process of grappling with and resolving moral issues.

Besides the purely physiological functions of the human digestive system, Hildegard explored its relation to the cosmos. She pointed out similarities between the macrocosm and the microcosm in terms of the extraction and absorption, the taking in and breaking down, the retention and elimination of substances that nourished people or caused them to waste away, elevated or stimulated them, irritated or caused them to fall ill. Only thus was Hildegard able to draw a proper analogy between the capacity of the stomach and that of the cosmos. "For everything in the universe fills up its storage space with whatever it sprouts or grows, only once again to become empty as its capacity dwindles. Similarly, humankind waxes and wanes like the moon and works with the soul which is filled with the elements of creation." Humanity was the true heart of nature "and a way leads from the heart to the elements which people use to accomplish what they contemplate." (CC 96)

After developing a scheme of the universe and a diagram of the human extremities, Hildegard proceeded next to the systematic description of people's sensory organs. She used the five senses to explain some of the body's amazing physical responses—hunger, sleep and fatigue—as well as its ability to assimilate, excrete and regenerate substances. Erecting a set of correspondences, Hildegard linked the senses to the world of the soul and the life of grace. She interpreted everything in the universe, down to the recesses of our conscience, in spiritual terms, thereby according them their proper significance. If Hildegard had not undertaken this daunting intellectual exercise, including every subject of her inquiry under three separate categories—the universe, the body, and the soul—she felt that we would never have gained access to the close relationship between the cosmos and its parts and humans and their component parts.

This same attitude is reflected in her "concept of the soul" which represented much more than just another contribution to medieval psychology or a different approach to the epistemology of scholasticism. Whenever Hildegard discussed the soul (*anima*), she was also referring to the body. She did not consider the seat of the soul to be either inside or outside the body. The soul existed in every part of the human organism and gave life to the body. The body and the soul were indispensable to each other; they were inextricably intertwined and coexisted in harmony. The soul was the active principle within the body (*opus corporis*); it rejoiced in its deeds and expressed itself though the body's activities (*opera corporis*). The purpose of the soul was to animate the body (*vita*) and cause things to happen (*opus*).

The primordial tree with its intricate arrangement of limbs branching out from a single trunk became a symbol for Hildegard of the primal unity of body, soul and spirit within humankind. "The soul in the body is like sap in a tree, and the soul's powers are like the form of the tree. And as the tree's form develops, so the soul reveals its powers. The intellect (*intellectus*) is like the greenery of the tree's branches and leaves, the will (*voluntas*) like its flowers, the mind (*animus*) like its bursting first fruits, and reason (*ratio*) like the perfected mature fruit. Finally, the senses (*sensus*) are comparable to the tree's size and shape. A person's body is strengthened and sustained by the soul." (Sc I, 4) The soul was the vivifying principle, and whatever the body did was an expression of the soul.

If you wish to understand the language of Hildegard's cosmology, you must take seriously the philosophy of nature, or better, the mystical approach to nature that underlay it. As the work of God (*opus operationis Dei*) humanity had a superior constitution and a preeminent place in the cosmos. God called upon human beings, as builders of creation (*homo operans*), to be the instruments of his creative power and, as a reflection of the cosmos (*speculum universi*), to help him complete his work. As rational beings (*homo rationalis*) people engaged in a permanent dialogue with the cosmos and thus became responsible for the created order and its message of salvation (*homo responsurus*). And just as God and humanity were, so to speak, "*one* in Christ" (*Deus et homo unus Christus*), the rational soul (*anima rationalis*) and the mortal flesh (*caro mortalis*) constituted one person (Sc II, 6).

By their nature the body and the soul work together in perfect harmony in the living entity that is the human being, in the same way that men and women are joined inseparably and sustain each other. Only male and female together constitute a complete human being.

This leads us to our next and probably most exciting chapter on medieval anthropology!

4. THE HUMAN BEING AS MALE AND FEMALE

If we wish to understand completely the nature of the body as the divine creation (*opus Dei*) it was meant to be, we must also accept the fact of sexuality along with its physiological and social aspects and its spiritual dimension.

Hildegard described the various stages or phases of human sexual behavior without a trace of prudishness. She assumed with her usual self-assurance that sex was an essential constituent of the primal state of humankind and formed an integral part of man's original make-up (*constitutio prima*). In the beginning male and female were created, in probity and not in baseness (*in honestate et non in turpitudine*), as sexual beings. Men and women joined in a bond of love (*in amore vivebant*) that was reflected in the conjugal act (*conjunctio*), a perfectly proper expression of love (*decenter instituta*). In *Causae et curae* Hildegard used imagery as charming as it was simple to describe the relationship between the sexes and the intimacy of sexual relations: "When God made Adam, God caused him to fall into a deep sleep and put a strong feeling of love in him. And God made a form for the love of man, and this is the way it came about that woman is the love of man. As soon as the woman was finished, God gave the man the power of begetting so that through his love, that is the woman, he could beget offspring. As soon as Adam's gaze fell upon Eve, he was immediately filled with wisdom because he saw before him the mother of his children. However, when Eve's glance fell upon Adam, she saw him as if she were looking up to heaven. For a soul that strives toward heaven looks to what is above; and her hope was placed in the man. In this way it came about that there is only one proper love between man and woman." (CC 136)

During sexual intercourse the man's semen combined with the woman's blood, and the blood of both became one flesh. "As soon as the male delivers his seed, it is accepted by the female's blood with all the desire of love and drawn into itself just as the breath draws something into itself. And so the man's seed blends with the female's blood and becomes a blood-like mixture and the female's flesh is nourished and grows and increases." (CC 67) In this fashion, the woman, through the desire of a particular male, truly became one flesh with man (*una caro cum viro de viro*).

Depending on their physical condition, males and females generally reached puberty when they were fifteen. The "storms of desire" began to subside between the ages of sixty and seventy, disappearing entirely around the age of eighty. Hildegard described in some detail the stages of sexual maturation, the moment of conception, defloration and the sexual act itself during which a female's "field" was furrowed by a male's "plow" until both partners' blood reached the boiling point and became mixed (*in unum confluunt*). Hildegard regarded the midpoint of the menstrual cycle as the optimum time for fertilization; on her "safe" days a woman's reproductive system was as dormant as a tree in winter.

Although men and women were equally disposed to engage in sex, profound differences in behavior took place after each had become aroused. A man's sexual desire could turn into a nearly unstoppable "volcanic eruption" during the heat of passion, and the force of his sexual drive was like a "wave breaking over a ship." A woman's libido, on the other hand, was more like an easily extinguishable fire in a woodpile, and her sexuality was analogous to the even heat of the sun. Hildegard praised the way in which women played down their intelligence and maintained their self-control. Women's erotic sensitivity was likened to their ability to "pick up even the slightest sound of a zither."

Hildegard also ascribed the differences between the sexes to the fact that Adam had acquired his virility from the earth's green life-force (*de viriditate virilis*) and his ability to beget children (*fortissimus*) by virtue of the elements; whereas Eve had been made out of Adam's rib, possessed a soft (*mollis*) body and had a kind of airy essence (*mens*). And since the world did not weigh as heavily upon Eve as it did upon Adam, she was more sensitive and possessed a talent for art, not to mention being a delightful and charming creature besides (*vita deliciosa*) (CC 46). Women were more fragile, but they were also more resilient than men, though they still needed a man's approval in order to undertake anything. Men were the natural protectors of women, but they had to court them in order to become their protectors. Women looked up to men and helped them in every way—woman was a reactive being. However because of Adam's sin, the deep sleep into which he fell—when taken together with the storm of passion that arose in him after Eve was taken from his rib— has often been interpreted as sleep of a different kind [the kind that occurs when man falls asleep with carnal desire].

Even now man had the same deep-seated urges, and—in the words of Psalm 42:1—"as the hart panteth after the water brooks," so man was still in swift pursuit of woman. Men and women clung to each other, pursued each other, provided warmth for each other, were sentimental and pas- sionate, and beguiled each other. They opened their hearts to and came to know each other, opened each other up and were initiated into each other's secrets. They constantly devised new names for each other, chal- lenged each other, and made excessive demands on each other. They responded to and complemented each other. And even though man was more productive, his creative power constituted only part of what a woman needed to be fulfilled. "Woman is a source of wisdom (*fons sapi- entiae*) and a fount of joy (*fons pleni gaudii*), a charming part of what man, with his greater creative power, needs in order to be fulfilled." (PL 167 B)

Typology of Sexual Behavior

As a biological entity the body was linked to the human personality chiefly through the sexual response. Love brought the various correspon- dences into consonance, and intimacy manifested itself in the physical encounter of two partners. This explains the surprisingly daring and detailed descriptions of sex that Hildegard presented to us—always in accord with the theory of "temperaments" developed during the age of classical antiquity. In describing the four temperaments—and then sepa-

rating them in characteristic fashion according to male and female—
Hildegard pointed out in each case the mixture of the four humors in the
brain and the nature of the vascular system as well as their relation to
musculature, skin color, and sexual potency. The four humors are briefly
described below.

First, Hildegard showed us sanguine men (CC 72/73). They had their
libido well under control while carrying out their sexual tasks, so that
their "stem blossoms and performs properly" (*ita quod etiam stirps
eorum in florem honorifice frondet*). In a proper embrace, they were
called the golden edifice (*aureum aedificium in recta amplexione*). When
they had no women with whom to interact, these men were as dull as a
day without sunshine.

Sanguine women had a propensity to become fat. They had soft, sump-
tuous flesh and delicate blood vessels that carried a rich supply of healthy
blood. They had a bright, white facial color. "They love tendernesses, are
kind, are exact in artistic work and are content with their lives. At the time
of menstruation, they suffer only a small loss of blood; their womb is well
developed for childbearing. If they live without mates and so bear no children, they easily become sick. However when they have husbands, they
are healthy." (CC 87)

Choleric men were hot-tempered. They felt robust and energetic when
they interacted with women. If they lived without a woman, they dried up,
and dragged themselves around like dying persons (*quasi moribundi*) or
engaged in perverse acts (CC 71). Choleric women, on the other hand,
were clever and charitable. They attracted men, but did not bind themselves to them. However if they were tied to a man, they were faithful and
remained healthy. If they did not have a husband, they suffered in body
(CC 88).

Phlegmatic men had broad, feeble blood vessels; their flesh was "soft
like a woman's flesh." They tried to pass themselves off as spirited, but
they lacked any real drive. They did not have the power to plow the earth
(*perfectionem aratri non habent*) because they could not interact with
women. And because they had this physical deficiency, they were also
slow of thought (CC 75/76). Phlegmatic women had serious faces,
swarthy skin, and a vacillating nature. Men attracted them, though, and
they were fruitful in producing posterity. They were difficult for others to

bear and excessive in their passion (CC 88).

Melancholic men were bitter and greedy. They were devious, subject to mental illness and largely unsuccessful with women. They were often dissolute in their passion and as unregulated in their interaction with women as a donkey (*sicut asini*). They often hated women and would have liked to kill the women with whom they were having sexual relations (CC 74). Melancholic women, in their turn, were heedless in their thoughts, often of foul disposition, and unstable. Since they could not receive or warm the male seed, they remained unfruitful. They were usually more healthy, more powerful, and happier (*saniores, fortiores et laetiores*) without a mate than with one. If they ever felt a desire of the flesh, it quickly passed (CC 89).

The Nature of Sexuality

Men and women were spiritually ordered toward each other and came together as sexual beings. This view, unambiguously expressed, was most unusual for the Middle Ages. Man and woman were so involved with each other that one of them was the work of the other (*sic ad invicem admisti sunt, ut opus alterum per alterum est*). Without woman, man could not be called man; without man, woman could not be named woman (LDO IV, 100: *quia vir sine femina vir non vocaretur, nec femina sine viro femina nominaretur*). Man and woman had obviously been created for each other (*propter virum creata—propter mulierem factus*). Therefore there was only one love (*una dilectio*). In any case, that was the way things were meant to be (CC 136).

The fact that "each of them was the work of the other" (*opus alterum per alterum*) was evidence of the concern of one gender for the other and took cognizance of the feminine side of man and the masculine side of woman. Love was more than mere nature, eros was more pleasurable than sex. Prominent theologians posited the idea that the purpose and meaning of cohabitation was not merely procreation, but rather the development of each partner as a living human being. When God created humankind, his intention was not to put an autonomous, self-sufficient creature into the world, just as he would not have been content to implant sexual organs into a purely spiritual being merely for the purpose of reproduction.

In God's total design, humans were created as sexual beings, in every part of their body and spirit. It was in sex that the human spirit came into full flower (*et in lumbis rationalitas floret*). This was how God created the human being at the beginning of time, and this was how God would restore his creature at the end of time—in his or her own body and gender (*in integritate membrorum et in sexu*). Man and woman responded as one (*sibi invicem responsum dant*); they lived together for their mutual happiness. Humans could never achieve complete joy by themselves alone. This joy had to be given to them by another human being: "But if one perceives the joy one receives from another person, one will feel in one's heart a great sense of enchantment (*exsultatio magna*). For then the soul will recall how it was created by God." (LDO VI, 5)

5. Working upon Nature

At the center of her scheme of the universe Hildegard saw the world in full bloom, a home to humanity the creator, an environment for human creativity. Through the months and seasons of the year people cultivated nature. The rhythms of life—every breath and pulse beat, the cycle of the days and nights through the months and years, the highs and lows during our brief time on earth and across the generations—served as guideposts for orienting people in the world. Life was change in the form of time. God had not only prefigured the natural world in the human sensuous figure, but the seasons as well. We matured as a function of the images of the world incorporated by us.

By these images Hildegard meant not only all natural phenomena but the phenomenon of culture and history as well. In both spheres she experienced the work of God (*operatio Dei*) as a noumenon and as an object of fascination. It was in this spirit that Hildegard experienced and described fire and water, the clouds and rivers, the stars and tempests, the moon and the night, a spring or a meadow, and always again that wondrously fresh and effervescent green life-force (*viriditas*), that is, everything that turned green, sprouted or bloomed.

Thus we read—to cite just one example—that the month of May symbolized sight. The eye was the prince of the sensory organs, and vision allowed people to appreciate "in a natural way how to use completely the

Figure 8. People cultivating the earth through the seasons of the year
(Cod. lat. 1942, Biblioteca Governativa Lucca, p. XIII)

things of nature." People were supposed to make use of whatever brought joy to them. This was the only way they could acquire a taste for the world, gain wisdom (*sapientia*), face the world responsibly, and obtain a genuine worldview, or view of the world. People were, after all, creatures of distinction and good taste (LDO IV, 98). They used their sense of taste to discern what would be most useful to strengthen their bodies.

In the same way, the ears were the seat of reason. Hearing represented, as it were, "the inception of the rational soul." The sense of smell was the arbiter between what was near and what was far; it was the repository of memory and scent, and at the same time the means of establishing a relationship, or of distancing oneself from someone or something. Proceeding in this same fashion through all the months of the year, Hildegard showed us how vast and lovely the world was when viewed through the eyes of a mature person who had a rational relation to nature. How else could God, the eternal One, become visible or be known, if he did not radiate brilliance? "For there is no creature without some kind of radiance—whether it be greenness or seeds, blossoms or another kind of beauty. Otherwise, it would not be a creature at all." (LDO IV, 11)

Nature in Revolt

Hildegard's relation to nature—she was, as it were, at peace with nature—derived initially from the idea of the primordial and inseparable connection between humanity and the cosmos, that is, a world in which organisms truly lived in harmony with one another and were integrated into their physical environment. If people behaved in the way they should, every season and the weather during every season would be the same: "This springtime would be just the same as previous springs, this summer just like past summers, and so on. However, since humankind because of its disobedience no longer fears or loves God, the elements and the seasons overstep their bounds." (CC 17) It was people's incessant quarreling (*inquieta bella*) that confused the elements. "Just as one holds a net in one's hand and shakes it, so humankind also brings the elements into motion, so that they, correspondingly, exercise their influence (*aura*) over human works." (CC 18/19)

For that reason—Hildegard wrote in horror—heaven and earth complained about humankind, for its restless behavior often put nature into a state of agitation, with disastrous consequences. The world was out of joint—so it seemed—since people began behaving like rebels in the created order. Only in this way was it possible for us to understand the "complaint of the elements" (*querela elementorum*) that Hildegard expressed in particularly dramatic terms when she let the elements speak for themselves, so that with "a loud voice" they exclaimed: "We cannot finish our natural orbit, for people turn us topsy-turvy just as a mill stone does. Therefore, we, the elements—air and water—stink with pestilence and hunger after all justice." (LVM III, 2)

The God-Man (*Vir Deus*) answered: "I will purge you with my branches and will torment people again and again until they return to me . . . The winds still stink with putrefaction, and the air vomits forth so much dirt that people do not dare open their mouth." Every creature, the response continued, clearly knew its creator. "Humanity, however, is a rebel (*homo rebellis*)! Humans alone divide their creator into a bewildering variety of creatures." (LVM III, 13) People blasphemed the earth that had drunk their blood; they polluted the air and obscured the light with this universal stench (*foeditas*) and this cosmic pestilence (*pestilentia*).

Humanity's cruel and relentless resistance to and rebellion against nature posed such a threat to the elements that they rose up in revolt. Things were not working as they normally did or as they were supposed to. Since the Creator filled up the world with various creatures for the service of humanity, they were ensnared by human disquiet (*inquietudo*) and displayed horrible terrors (*horribiles terrores*). "All the elements and all creatures cry aloud at the blaspheming of nature and at wretched humankind's devotion of so much of its short life to the rebellion against God; whereas unthinking nature submissively carries out the divine laws. This is why nature complains so bitterly about humanity."

In her commentary on "The Complaint of the Elements," Hildegard described in some detail how closely people were associated with nature and how intimately they were involved with the elements, "in the same way as the elements are in league with humanity." Confused by human behavior, the elements went beyond the bounds established by nature and were swept up in unnatural acts, with all the consequences that followed from acts of perversion (LVM III, 31). People not only shared in this "universal stench," they were also responsible for putting nature off balance. Hildegard used the impurity of the air, crop failures, illnesses, and weather-related disasters to illustrate her point. "And I saw how the outer fire of the firmament rained down torrents of filth and garbage on the earth, giving rise to festering sores and ghastly tumors in human and animal and plant. I also saw how fog descended upon the earth from the sphere of black fire (*ignis niger*) and dried up the greenness and fruits of the fields. I saw too how another fog descended upon the earth from the sphere of pure white air destroying both human and beast." (LVM III, 34) And again: "The fire sends forth ferocious noises. The wind and air issue a blast with whirlwinds. To the accompaniment of thunder and lightning and with rain splashing everywhere, they hurl exceedingly sharp stones into the cosmos." (Sc I, 3)

Duty toward Nature

Using "The Complaint of the Elements," that is, the charges leveled by the elements, Hildegard sought to show how people's duty on earth— their work upon creation (*opus cum creatura*)—was a fundamentally ecological task. What she meant by this was that people were capable of transforming nature, of reshaping and altering it while bringing its—and ultimately their own—potentialities to reality. According to the divine plan (*oikonomia*), humanity was, as it were, immersed in nature, and the elements were an integral part of history. These were far-reaching views for the time and could easily have led to the development of a "philosophy of nature" and a "theology of work."

Given their biological structure and their personal consciousness, people were clearly capable of communing with the cosmos. "The elements," the *Praefatio* to the *Physica* stated, "willingly served humanity because they sensed that people were endowed with life. They cooperated in human enterprises and worked with people, just as people worked with them." (PL 1125 A) The elements of the world, after all, had been "created for the service of humanity." (Sc I, 3)

Human beings failed in their cosmic mission. They forfeited their work (*opus*) and were doomed by the Word (*verbum*). They became humanity the rebel (*homo rebellis*) who, having failed (*destitutio*), brought the elements into confusion and upset the flow of time. The firmament began to revolve and purge the polluted elements. Time revolved in cycles, heading for its ultimate conclusion. All the elements were wrapped in a great darkness and remained there. After Adam's fall human beings were sent into exile to earn their living by the sweat of their brow (CC 46): they began the arduous task of working with this recalcitrant world.

Yet people faced the world squarely; it was familiar to them, and they could communicate with other human beings within it. Hence their ability to know the world. Special note must be taken of this cosmological dimension in an age in which all "nature" has been reduced to scientific models, in which anything "spiritual" is validated only in terms of abstract concepts or depth psychology, and in which the "world" as such has virtually nothing to do with the image of humanity. Humanity's work space, however, is not limited to the soul or spirit alone, and it is not located solely in the realm of nature or technology. The true human being as a totality continues to have a physical impact upon its world.

What Hildegard presented us with in her image of humanity was a coherent "philosophy of the body human." Humankind was God's handiwork (*opus Dei*) and had a duty to work upon creation (*opus cum creatura*) and to cooperate with others (*opus alterum per alterum*). The human being therefore personified the key concepts of Hildegard's physiology, pathology and therapy. We will examine these subjects in more detail as we proceed through natural history to the field of medicine.

IV

Natural History and the Healing Arts

Prefatory Remarks

Hildegard's highly original contributions to natural history and medicine were an integral part of her views of humanity and the world. It would be as absurd to separate them from her lifework and include them under the rubric of traditional folk medicine, as it would be simply to classify them as part of her visionary writings and call them "divine medicine." It is a testimony to the logic of Hildegard's thought processes and her remarkable sense of reality that, through her magnificent visions of the spiritual duties of human beings, she also sought to understand their physical being in health and disease, that is, the concrete reality of their everyday life.

What Abbot Ildefons Herwegen (1930) regarded as characteristic of and admired most in Hildegard's natural history and medicine was the "extraordinary love of the cosmos" they manifested. He noted that there was "no other medieval person who came anywhere near to attaining her profound understanding of the invisible web of nature or her universal empathy with the elements of creation." It is from the vantage point of this fundamental love of nature that we must examine her written contributions to natural history.

Composed between 1150 and 1160, Hildegard's writings on natural history and medicine stand in sharp contrast to her three visionary theological works. We have based our discussion of Hildegard's *Causes and Cures* on the 13th century manuscript preserved in the Kongelige Bibliotek in Copenhagen (Ny. kgl. saml. 90b) and published under the title *Hildegardis Causae et curae*. The text—as well as Hildegard's *Physica*, of which several manuscripts have come down to us—is supposedly part of an older work entitled *Liber subtilitatum diversarum naturarum creaturarum* (*The Subtleties of the Diverse Natures of Created Things*).

Figure 9. After the Fall, *homo rebellis*
stymies the act of creation
(Cod. lat. Ms. 1 (ca. 1165), Hessische
Landesbibliothek Wiesbaden, *Scivias* I, 2)

Given the growing interest in "Hildegardian medicine," we must keep in mind the fact that her writings on natural history derived from her personal experiences with nature and reflect the state of knowledge of her time. It is as difficult to identify diseases from the names used in her time as it is to recognize the plants and remedies to which she referred. Thus all attempts to apply naturopathy—a perfectly legitimate system of treatment in its own right—to the practice of medicine and pharmacy under the guise of "Hildegardian Medicine" have absolutely no basis in science.

Despite all the praiseworthy contributions of her contemporaries to the advancement of the healing arts, I still believe that Hildegard is the most outstanding representative of the spirit of medieval medicine. We see preserved in her work all the constituents of a tradition that had developed organically: the customs of antiquity and elements of folklore, the discipline of scholasticism and the practical experience of monastic medicine. Hildegard pretended to be merely an ordinary human being (*simplex homo*) who would never dare to challenge the famous masters of the schools of Salerno or Toledo, Chartres or Paris, even though she far outshone them all in terms of intellect and charisma.

1. The Workings of Nature

To this learned 12th-century abbess nature was not a rigidly defined area of objectifed experience. Rather, "nature" was the repository of a world of symbols that was communicated to people directly through the elements—in stones and in the stars, through plants and animals. All the elements served humanity; they worked with people as people worked with them. "In this reciprocal arrangement the earth released its life-determining force (*viriditas*) according to the particular type and nature of human being involved, its mode of thinking and way of life." (PL 1125 A)

We still have a sense here of the planting of Eden: God's presence as the Creator; the flowering garden that "is pleasant to the sight" of the Lord and to the sight of humankind who looked up in amazement, who read the book of nature, interpreted all its signs, talked with all things, just as they addressed people. But we also have a sense of the natural world that God had entrusted to human beings, that shared their fate after the fall, that reflected their sadness in its lamentations and expressed the hope of being called back to its Creator. To Hildegard the spiritual purpose of nature was to be God's dwelling place in the created order.

Causae et curae begins by stating that God was and is without beginning, that he was and is the brilliant light, and that he was and is life (CC 1). It was out of his pure goodness that God the Father made the world and that at the center of the world he placed humanity, which had all of creation within it (CC 2). God put all creation under humanity, "so that they might master it with their virile power (*penetrare*) and so that they might know and understand everything. Humanity contains all of creation (*homo omnis creatura*), and the breath of life that never dies is in humanity." (CC 45) God placed humanity on earth like an "exquisite jewel" (*elegantissimum lapidem*) so that "all of creation would see itself reflected in humanity's radiance." (LVM I, 83)

Because of their sins people became fragile creatures (*homo destitutus*), frail, sickly, and mortal. In striving to be autonomous beings (*superbia*) they severed his relations with nature and became rebels (*homo rebellis*) forced to bear their inner conflicts throughout history. Disease was the outward sign of depression and insanity, and Hildegard interpreted it as an excessive increase in black bile (*melancolia*). Melancholy, however, was constantly countered by greenness (*viriditas*), a natural life-determining force that restored people to health (*homo restitutus*).

A nun skilled in the art of healing, Hildegard coined a term to encompass the lush green of life in all of nature's creations as well as the healing powers of the organism, health, and the vitality of the spirit. The term she chose was "greening power" (*viriditas*) which in a mysterious way was inherent "in animals and fishes and birds, in all plants and flowers and trees," in all the beautiful things of this world (LDO IV, 11).

At first Hildegard viewed greening power in strictly naturalistic terms and in the context of the elements. It manifested itself in grasses and plants and was sustained by the four elements, by fire, earth, water, and air. It moistened stones, shimmered in the water, glowed in fire, and was especially refreshing when carried by the breezes from which "the grass in early morning takes in greenness as eagerly as a lamb takes in milk." In the typical symbolist manner of interpreting meaning on more than one level of reference, she abstracted the images of greenness from their natural environment and used them to evoke a world beyond that known to ordinary sense, to the intellect. This is why Hildegard was able to maintain that human flesh was green and that blood possessed a special greening power. Everything that we refer to as the "soul" and Hildegard called the "life force of the body" was green. The color green shone with particular brightness whenever sex was involved, whether it was a man's sexual prowess (*virilitas*) or germinating fruit. The greenness of a woman's blood showed when she was fertile and revealed with particular clarity the vital essence of her femininity (*viriditas floriditatis feminae*). Even human reason (*rationalitas*), human knowledge (*scientia*) and, most especially, human conscience (*conscientia*) were green in color.

It speaks highly of the intellectual courage of this medieval woman that she was never content with conventional symbols and that time and again she transcended her own vision of the cosmos, putting it on an eschatological plane. Thus it is no accident that nature's manifest greening power became a mirror image of the greenness that lay hidden at the heart of eternity. In a kind of hermeneutic spiral, the images steadily increased in intensity as they ascended to the heights of transcendence.

This is why Hildegard could say: "There is a power in eternity, and it is green." This mysterious greenness colored the entire course of salvational history. It was active in Abraham, the father of fertility, and it revealed itself in Christ who was made human in the "green womb" of the Virgin, overshadowed by the Holy Spirit. And it was the Holy Spirit who gave human beings the gift of that green space from which they were prepared to respond in word and deed. So we should not be surprised to find this key concept appear in of all places Hildegard's *Causae et curae*: *opus verbi viriditas est* (the work of the Word is greening power). The work of God the Father in the Word of the Son was the bright green power of the Spirit, and the reality of the Word was verdant life!

God created heaven and earth out of the bright green life force, and all the world's beauty blossomed forth out of the Holy Spirit, the root of all created being. "This Spirit purges the world of all impurities. All guilt is erased, all pain eased, every wound soothed. Thus the Spirit is Life, radiant praiseworthy Life, Life that arouses all things and reawakens the cosmos."

From the lowest-lying land to the loftiest light the green life-determining force sent its beams, like the branches of an enormous tree, into the heavens, far beyond the sun and the moon and the stars. Even in our desiccated times that have lost the ability to create, it appeared out of the immense greenness of paradise, turning everything green and growing right up to the beautiful emerald gates of the heavenly Jerusalem. It was from this perspective that Hildegard viewed the spirit of the cosmos dashing through history to put greening power in motion: "Thus God's reality is never in vain. None of his work remains fruitless; it all comes back completed. God's Word is heard and answered. The Spirit goes out, grows, and produces fruit. This is life!"

Hence nature per se was never really home to us, never truly an "ideal world." Nature needed the intervention of humanity with the gift of reason to shape and give it direction. As God's creatures human beings were capable of working creatively and fashioning their own world. With these ideas to guide us, we can elucidate Hildegard's basic contributions to physiology and pathology. Hildegard regarded disease not as a pathogenic process, but as the result of deficiencies and neglect (*modus deficiens*), of the lack or absence of something; whereas the creative process (*creatio*) was attributable to that state of health which derived its creative power from the green life-force (*viriditas*) that was part of the process by which God had set the world in motion and held out hope to a nature bereaved that it would someday be recalled by its Creator to live in eternity.

2. The Basis and Nature of Disease

It would be impossible to understand medieval medicine without a knowledge of the theory of the elements and the humors, fully developed during classical antiquity by Hippocrates and Galen. It was an all-encompassing theory that included the four elements and the four humors, the four forces and the four qualities as well as the four temperaments. Taken together, they determined the physical and mental state of a person in health and disease.

Isidore of Seville early pointed out the relationship of the four elements to the four humors that cause illness in human beings: "All diseases arise from the four humors, namely, blood, yellow bile, black bile, and phlegm. They keep healthy persons in balance and cause harm to those who are sick." (*Etymologiae* IV, 5) So long as the mixture of the humors was in equilibrium with respect to heat and moisture—wrote Hildegard as well—the individual was blessed with a healthy mind in a healthy body. However when the humors seriously diverged from their original or ideal proportions, one fell sick.

Because of the essential complexity of the system of humors, one humor often predominated over the others producing signs of physical or mental illness. The enormous variation in dispositions could be explained in terms of the varying proportions of the four humors, so that we might speak of a typology of temperaments—similar to those we described in discussing sexual behavior—or likewise of a typology of diseases.

There were hard-hearted people (*homines duri*) who were self-centered, had little regard for others and became intemperate when they fell ill. There were others who had an airy (*aeri*) temperament and were correspondingly fickle. And there were still others who possessed an unruly disposition (*quasi turbo*); they were uncontrollable and inconsolable. Finally, there was another type that had a passionate disposition (*ardentes*); they were restless and easily alienated in both health and disease (Bw 180).

The elements, together with their corresponding qualities, created a link to the forces of the external world, symbolized by the winds and the planets which exercised their influence through animal heads. Here is one example of the way in which Hildegard described the function of the humors in the body. At times, she wrote, they raged as fiercely as a leopard, and then they became calm, like a crab that sometimes crawled forward and at other times backward. The humors showed their contrariness in the leaping and stamping of the stag which, when weary, sought diversion in vain things. In the form of the crab, the humors warned people to move forward with caution, and then they plunged them again into doubt. In the form of the stag, they lulled them into a sense of security and caused them to vacillate. "Such thoughts attack a person sometimes like a ravenous wolf and at other times like a stag or a crab." (LDO III, 9)

In this way the humors that flowed through the body confused people's thoughts and emotions and attacked the individual organs on a grand scale. An especially good example of this phenomenon was the spleen which according to the ideas of the ancients was the source of "black bile," which in its turn was the cause of numerous symptoms indicative of illness. What was now "bile" in the human body shined like a crystal before Adam's fall "and had the taste of good work in it. What is now black bile in people lighted like the dawn and had consciousness and the completion of good works in it." After Adam's fall this brilliance was darkened and changed to bitterness. "And so Adam was completely transformed (*totus mutatus*). Hence his soul became sad." (CC 145)

Human beings had essentially forfeited their original status; they became sickly and frail. They now led lives of fear and sorrow. Any greening power (*viriditas*) that was still active in them grew pale and faded, revealing a panoply of imperfections. Humankind appeared irresolute (*homo mutabilis*) in its perplexity (*diversa incertitudo*), burdened with the vices of restlessness (*vitia instabilitatis*) and a wandering mind (*evagatio mentis*), at the crossroads of earthly cares (*in quadruvio curarum saecularium*), menaced in their "shipwrecked world." We were blinded and blind and bereft of security (*nullam securitatem*). Our own actions had become puzzling and problematical to us (*omnia opera incerta*). Thus humanity's days passed (*mones dies deficiendo*) and were forgotten (*in oblivionem ducuntur*).

It was against this existentially unstable backdrop that Hildegard related her own experiences with sickness. Time and again we learn she suffered from "serious illnesses that confined her to bed." She was never able to rid herself of a "restless trembling" that she frequently wrote about when describing herself. She felt "greatly hampered" by her illnesses and "racked by pains" that threatened to kill her. Since sorrow and grief pierced her body and soul, she often thought she was going to die. From her earliest childhood she had never been free from anxiety, "never, not one hour." She described a pain so "great and overwhelming that it shattered all faith and solace." And yet in spite of all this she dealt creatively with sickness and suffering, and in the end she retained her faith in the possibility of recovery: "Like a mother who has just given birth, I can once again talk about my pain" (PL 128B: *et sicut pariens post laborem, ita loquebar post dolorem*).

Hildegard sought to encapsulate her own basic pathology when she confessed: "I, wretched creature, am lacking in health (*sanitas*), strength (*vis*), stamina (*fortitudo*), and learning (*doctrina*) . . ." I am but a shadow of life's power, truly a long-suffering human being (*homo patiens*) who has been received by Christ the physician, the great physician (*magnus medicus*) "who rouses those who are awake, shakes those who are asleep, and plunges those who persist in evil into the abyss." (PL 350 B) Thus Hildegard warned Abbot Bertulf in a letter not to become complacent: Take care of your own so long as you have eyes, "for the good physician (*bonus medicus*) does not hesitate to treat people's wounds with compassion." (PL 287 B/C) The letter concluded: Therefore wake up and bear your burdens!

3. THE MEANS OF HEALING AS THE MEANS TO SALVATION

The "healing arts" in the work of this saintly woman indicated in broad outline the way in which scholastic medicine, drawing on Greek and Arabic sources, was to develop during her lifetime. According to the paradigm of scholasticism, medical theory dealt with logic, physics, and ethics, and medical practice with dietetics, pharmacy, and surgery. However other equally important areas of medicine were already clearly discernible in Hildegard's *Causae et curae*, where natural history (*res naturales*), the study of life (*res non naturales*), and the conduct of life (*moralia*) were also the subjects of medicine. What motivated the healing arts was the desire to optimize a person's ability to conduct his or her life while also deriving pleasure from and enjoying the healing process and everything associated with it (*integritas*).

It was in this spirit that for thousands of years people skilled in the healing arts used substances of medicinal value borrowed from the external world, i.e., the animal, plant, and mineral kingdoms (*materia medica*). With great reverence people viewed medicinal remedies as "God's hands" coming to console those appealing for help. The means of salvation were often indistinguishable from the medicinal means used to restore health. These *pharmaka*—meaning drugs, whether healing or noxious, that is, poisonous—could be prescribed only as part of a strict hierarchy of treatment. Surgery was the last resort. Before that came the application of remedial substances (*materia medica*). At the beginning of the process stood a physician who generally prescribed diet therapy (*regimen sanitatis*).

Hildegard's description of diseases and their treatment (*Causae et curae*) must be considered first within the framework of humoral pathology. Hildegard the physician adhered strictly to indications that had been handed down from the past and to traditional treatments that seemed most reasonable to her. She was familiar with the plusses and minuses of various remedies (*juvamenta et nocumenta*), used them with extreme caution, and recommended treatment guardedly on a case-by-case basis. The natural substances that the Creator had tailored to the needs of humankind were of benefit only when they were used according to strict guidelines, that is, only when reasonable and necessary (*rationabili necessitate*) and with discretion (*discrete*).

Hildegard found new uses for natural remedies. She recommended using water with its wondrous powers in a systematic manner, not merely for bathing. She pointed to the existence of spices hidden on the ocean floor that possessed great healing power and yet were still inaccessible to man. And she wrote about the coolness of the blue lily that helped keep the libido in check and about the leaves of the apple tree in springtime that were as tender as young maidens and equally beneficial.

For a remedy to be effective a patient had to cooperate in his or her treatment and focus on the natural way of life dictated by people's common sense. The rules for leading a disciplined and properly balanced life had not been established, as the wise abbess pointed out, to inconvenience people. Rather, we should take pleasure in and enjoy pursuing the rational way of life. The rules of life were meant as a support, not a burden.

As we move further into this "house of healing," we encounter a complete inventory of remedies (*ratio sanationis*) which are listed in detail according to the standard criteria of pharmaceutical science—potions and poultices, rinses and fumigants as well as all manner of other preparations along with their ingredients and medical applications. (The medical historian Irmgard Müller wrote a paper for a 1979 Festschrift published on the 800th anniversary of Hildegard's death in which she examined various categories of disease and the remedies used to treat them.)

Although Hildegard borrowed a number of traditional prescriptions and treatments, they all bore the stamp of her personal experiences (PL 1125–1127). There was always a certain aura, the sense of an intellect that was cognizant of the unity of humanity and the cosmos, nature and habitat. Thus the healing power of plants was mainly a function of their primordial vitality or greenness (*viriditas*). If a plant was very green, you only had to touch a patient with it, which was comparable to the homeopathic practice of prescribing only highly diluted doses of drugs. In cases of myopia the mere sight of a bright green meadow was said to have a therapeutic effect.

In the early Middle Ages this naturalistically ordered cosmology was enhanced by the addition of a moral principle of therapy based on caring and love. Thus the healing arts in Western Christendom far surpassed the medical techniques of antiquity. From medicine that was purely a craft (*techne therapeutike*) there developed a religion of healing that ministered to the sick (*diakonia*) and was sustained by a spirit of compassion and mercy (*misericordia*). The first thing a physician would do in coming to the aid of a patient who was longing to be cured was to treat him or her with the compassion that one human being was always ready to show to another. Thus the "voice of God" said to Hildegard: "I am the great Physician (*magnus medicus*) and act like a doctor who sees a sick person who longs to be cured." (Sc I, 3) Mercy was invariably directed toward the other person (*flectens se ad hominem*); it was a profound feeling for the suffering and personal tragedy of another (*miseriis compatiens*). It imitated the mercy of the Good Samaritan (*imitans Samaritanum*) and personified love of neighbor (*cooperiens hominem*) (Sc III, 3).

If it were not for *misericordia*, hard-heartedness (*obduratio cordis*) would run rampant (*sine misericordia bacchantur duritiae*). Thus, mercy had a very special role to play in orienting man in his world, for what in large measure characterized the "world" was coldness and selfishness, that is, hard-heartedness. Hard-heartedness appeared to us in Hildegard's *Liber Vitae Meritorum* (*Book of the Rewards of Life*) as a figure that moved neither up nor down but remained motionless. It stared into the darkness with its large black eyes and said: "I created nothing; I established nothing. Why, therefore, should I do any work or wear myself out for anyone else? I will leave things as they are! Let God who created all things take care of these things! Why should I pay attention to all the happy and sad people? I will take care of myself. Let others take care of themselves!" (LVM I, 16)

The figure of Mercy (*misericordia*) responded to the words of Selfishness, cold and hard as stone, by pointing to all the beauty in the world: "Flowering plants give out an aroma to other plants and a stone shines on other stones. All creation has a primordial urge to embrace in love. All the creatures on earth minister to humans and by doing this joyfully and with love they accomplish good." Hence "Mercy" continued: "My heart is so full that I can give to others. I think about what is needed and I do that. I help all the sick get healthy. I am like salve for every pain and my words are a balm." (LVM I, 17)

It was primarily the Virgin Mary, the "bright mother of the sacred art of healing," the "artist of life," "radiant in every fullness of joy," "sweet in all the fullness of bliss," who poured balsam on the wounds of mortals. This was how in many of her songs Hildegard extolled the Virgin, the "mother of medicine" (*mater medicinae*). It was Mary who endowed us with mercy, the best possible medicine (*magna medicina*), an "exceedingly sweet plant in the air and dew and all green freshness." A remedy's effectiveness (*fortitudo*) was a function of *misericordia* cloaked in the greenness of the life force (*viriditas*). Mercy was called "the King's loveliest paramour." According to Hildegard we would have to face the "evil of evils" (*pessimum malum malorum*) if things should ever reach the point "where people are no longer concerned with the health of their neighbors and have no compassion for their fellow human beings."

It was mercy alone that made of the heart a pure spring. "The more one achieves mastery over oneself through true self-discipline, the more prepared one is, with charity in one's heart, to help a neighbor in need." Did not God himself, after all, treat people with mercy, attend to their afflictions, fill our cups with the "wine of atonement" and "anoint us with mercy." (LDO V, 46) Whoever was weighed down by vices should seek God's mercy. Confession, repentance and atonement were a second resurrection (Sc II, 6: *confessio secunda resurrectio est*). All that was foul was eliminated, as it were, with deep repentance, in the same way that digested food and drink were eliminated (LDO IV, 85).

Penitence—the refreshing green power of healing (*viriditas poenitentiae*)—appeared in Hildegard's medical works as the "light of the soul" and as a remedy [of purgation] (*quasi medicina*). It set people in motion, stirred them deeply, taught them to open up, to come to their senses, and by looking into their hearts to change their ways. Penitence was an all-powerful force. The spirit of penitence yearned to be effective at all times, just as—in a typical Hildegardian analogy—woman yearned to put herself at the disposal of man through her knowledge and abilities. "Man, who was created strong and powerful in the likeness of God, will fulfill all his work together with woman, who was the cause of man's downfall but through whom all that is evil will be restored for the better."

Beginning in the shattered human heart, the healing power of penitence led people out of their tribulations and back to life. Tears refreshed them and made them free again; tears made hard hearts soft and summoned the Holy Spirit. They caused *viriditas*—that refreshing and rejuvenating, creative green life force whose radiance rose to the Divine Light—to once again well up in the human soul.

4. THE HEALING ARTS AS A GUIDE TO THE ART OF LIVING

For half a millennium medieval doctors, inspired by the Rule of St. Benedict, advised and treated Western Europeans. However they never produced their own body of professional literature, developed surgical techniques or established academies; and virtually no outstanding physicians rose from their ranks. Yet they passed down to us precisely what modern medicine, with all its technical achievements, lacks most—the concept of the patient, specific ways to lead a healthy life, and the obligation on the part of the physician to attest to a patient's recovery and health.

At the center of Hildegardian medicine there stood the figure of a suffering person who wished to be made whole again. The figure appeared before us larger than life and as a coherent whole: body and soul in one being; created in the primordial conditions of paradise; living in disgrace due to its own transgressions; yet destined to attain eternal well-being and salvation. Hildegard viewed the lives of human beings within their fragile physical shell, their day-to-day relationship with their frail bodies—in sum, all the tribulations of our lives—as opportunities to triumph over time and eternity and take on the enormous task of working upon the world and cultivating nature in health and disease.

In such an age of upheaval and disorientation as the late Middle Ages,

Hildegard realized that the time had come to move systematically via the way of nature toward a systematic plan for living. Now, Hildegard wrote to Manegold, Abbot of Hirsau, was "the time to fight for the conduct of human life." (Bw 130) We cannot emphasize strongly enough the specificity of Hildegard's rules of conduct. They ultimately represented nothing less than the deliberate structuring of every aspect of daily living, which in its turn was primarily the task of the healing arts, although not exclusively, for a day meant more than simply the events that filled it. Ultimately, the day became for Hildegard a symbol of the history of salvation.

In a letter to the canons of the cathedral at Mainz, the aged abbess compared the various periods of the day to the stages of salvational history. "O true Love," she wrote, "You Eternal God! You made humankind in such a short span of time for all your other so wisely created creatures and led them, as it were, to an already well-laid table. The day breaks, it is said, when the first flush of dawn precedes the sunrise. Straightaway you breathed the breath of life into humanity, just as the sun that follows the dawn immediately shines forth its brilliant rays. The breath of life, the soul, is a fire whose flame is reason, by which all the powers of the soul to apprehend good and evil are known, just as the sun is known by its brilliance." (PL 222 B)

Having set the proper mood, Hildegard expanded her analogy in phases to encompass her cosmology and eschatology: "The hour during which God put Adam into the garden of Eden and showed him the delights of paradise was equivalent to the first three hours [of the day]. The time it took Adam to name every living creature and fowl of the air filled hours three through six. During this time God appeared to Adam only against the backdrop of the morning sun, so that Adam could not make out his countenance and saw only a certain radiance." And the Lord caused a deep sleep to fall upon Adam and lifted his spirit to the pinnacle of knowledge. God showed him how his offspring would someday fill the heavenly Jerusalem.

The same hour that God made Adam sleep, He took a rib out of him and fashioned a woman from it. "When this woman was brought to him and he recognized her, Adam was greatly pleased." (PL 222 D) Soon, however, the day of salvation drew to a close. When Adam and Eve were driven from paradise and into the world, they found that night had descended upon the earth. "However they discovered there everything that suited their human nature, everything that was necessary for life (*necessaria*), for themselves as well as for all other creatures, and they learned to use everything for their own purpose." (PL 223 A)

They learned to use all the things that were naturally available to them, that is, all the necessities of life that we take for granted and that nevertheless have to be carefully cultivated: breathing and eating and drinking, work and relaxation, sleeping and waking, as well as all the passions and joys that are part of our arduous daily lives. God also endowed us with personal needs so that we could learn to appreciate what did us good and to look forward to what was useful (LVM IV, 12: *unde homo praevidebat, quid sibi prosit*). Simply put, people were responsible for their own prosperity, an adequate standard of living, and a lifestyle that was to become more humane with every passing day.

Just as Hildegard viewed life as a continuation of creation (*creatio continua*), she regarded health as a process of continual regeneration drawing upon the very wellsprings of life, an ongoing life-giving process that embraced and overlay all the spheres of nature and the spirit. The aim of life was to produce a well-rounded person. Surprisingly, Hildegard used the life of Jonathan in the Old Testament to illustrate her concept of the model human being who was spiritually and physically in perfect equilibrium: "Jonathan might be compared to rich and fertile soil that is easily plowed up and while being plowed creates the conditions for medicinal plants to grow. He was reserved and mellow in manner (*mitis in moribus*). His judgments were genuine and just, and he displayed neither hatred nor anger. In those of similar disposition the humors are, through the foods they eat, perfect in quality and quantity (*sani et optimi*) and well mixed throughout the body—in the brain, the blood vessels, and the marrow. Anger and sadness have no chance to gain ground in such people, for God's grace causes them to sprout and grow, just as the dew brings forth greenery from the earth. People of like disposition display an abundance of well-being in all their actions. Their flesh grows and their blood supply increases through eating, and they therefore maintain their vitality." (PL 1050 C)

For this way of life everything that happened in the course of a day—work and relaxation, eating and fasting, talking and silence—depended on the maintenance of a steady rhythm. Everything was symbolic of the fact that the development (*doctrina*) of the inner person helped to form and shape the outer person. And while people's strictly outward behavior (*conversatio*) affected their daily habits, their inner transformation (*conversio*) lifted them out of the present and swept them into the realm of eternity.

Aside from the prosaic work of structuring day-to-day life, the Abbess Hildegard worked out specific guidelines to cover every phase of her charges' maturation. She wanted them to grow like trees, so that their spiritual powers, as well as their blood and marrow, would attain quiet stability (*stabilitas*) and constancy (*constantia*), that is, undergo a permanent transformation (*conversio morum*). A person could develop only under conditions of constancy and in the tranquility of a self-contained setting. All her medical knowledge and ambitions aside, Hildegard offered a new and far-reaching view of pedagogy. She even interpreted doctrine from the standpoint of our personal lives. She compared the teacher to a bird feeding its young: "The teacher has to pick and choose words like a loving mother so that the pupils will open their mouths wide and swallow the knowledge proffered." From time to time the teacher had to establish stricter rules, and "like a headmaster let [pupils] feel the sting of the cane and then like a physician treat their wounds with salve." Using just the stick, however, and not the carrot meant that the pupils would never be nourished. On the other hand, "when teachers have only nice-sounding words to offer their pupils, the pupils will never learn."

Hildegard once took to task an abbot at the monastery of St. Matthias in Trier and, using agricultural and horticultural imagery, admonished him to moderate his lifestyle: "Drench your soul in the water brooks of Scripture and the lives of the saints . . . Do all these things with humility, cause flowers to bloom on your brothers as they do on the branches of trees. Be a sun through your teaching, a moon through your kindness, be like the wind in the firmness of your behavior, like a mild breeze in your gentleness, and like fire in the eloquence of your teaching. Begin all these things at the first crimson light of dawn and complete them in the brilliant light of day." During the daytime such a teacher functioned as the pupils' eyes, and at night the teacher stayed with them like a vigilant guardian (PL 289 A).

In Hildegard's works the art of living and the art of healing were inextricably intertwined and subject to the same rules. Hildegard regarded the idea of submitting oneself to strict rules for living—rules, she emphasized, that one either imposed on oneself (*sive per ipsum*) or accepted from an outside source (*sive per alium*)—as part of a rational lifestyle. This is a perfectly natural path for humanity to follow (LDO IV, 73: *et hoc ei naturale est*), for all nature naturally aspires to be brought under cultivation.

5. THE WAY OF NATURE AND THE CONDUCT OF LIFE

The underlying principles of a healthy lifestyle are readily assembled from among the many writings that comprise Hildegard's extensive oeuvre. The most concise presentation of these principles is found in her explication of the Benedictine Rule (*Explanatio Regulae S. Benedicti*). In the introduction to her detailed commentary on the Rule (PL 1055–1066), Hildegard described herself as a wretched woman (*paupercula feminea forma*) untutored in scholarship (*magisterium humanum*), a woman who saw herself as an instrument of the Holy Spirit. It was in this same spirit of humility that Benedict had composed his Rule (*doctrina regulae*). Hildegard compared him to a secret spring (*fons clausa*) from which doctrine flowed in outstanding discretion. Whenever this gentle ecclesiastic decided to hammer in the nail of doctrine (*clavum doctrinae*), he never aimed too high or too low and always managed to hit the center of the wheel of life (*medium rotae*). Thus anyone—the strong and the weak alike—could, as their abilities allowed, slake their thirst at Benedict's spring. The Rule reflects the spirit of moderation that was a determining factor in the way Benedict divided the working day.

Although Hildegard's commentary on the Rule of St. Benedict focused on the norms for monastic living, it also elucidated the saint's highly detailed instructions regarding clothing, food, sleep, etc. However, it is only when the commentary is taken together with her other writings that we begin to understand her systematic approach to the monastic way of life which was based on the themes of classical hygiene and dietetics. As we delve into these various topics, we learn how and why our days and lives were shaped by physical facts and bodily needs: light and air, eating and drinking, work and relaxation, waking and sleeping, not to mention our emotional ups and downs.

The first topic of her commentary covered the way in which people dealt with nature—with light and air, water and warmth, soil and climate, with the envelope that surrounded the earth and in which we lived our lives. This was the "world" as seen through the eyes of medieval people, a world composed of the elements—fire, air, earth and water—which formed our puny bodies and helped sustain us during the course of our lives. God placed humanity in adequate surroundings, and humanity then had to adapt to them (PL 1062 A). However, just as people were dependent on the atmosphere, so the environment was forever subject to human influence.

Hildegard used the image of a revolving wheel (*rota*), encircled by moving layers of air that bolstered and energized life, to illustrate this "ecosystem." "The air sends forth dew and causes everything that is green to sprout, sets the breath of the wind in motion, entices the blossoms to burst forth, spreads warmth, so that everything will ripen fully"—in an atmosphere of truly healthy living. The layers of air and the waterways endowed the earth with the same fruitfulness that the soul bestowed on the body (LDO IV, 16). Everything described here was rich in symbolism. The fowl of the air stood for people's ability to produce plans based on their thoughts, while the beasts in the field symbolized the translation of his ideas into vigorous action.

The firmament's upper fire, however, brought devastating burns and wounds (*stigmata et ulcera*) to human and animal as well as to the fruits of the earth (LDO IV, 1). Hildegard clearly described how air and water pollution and ecological disasters could happen when the elements were unable to complete their appointed journeys because of the interference of humanity, the "cosmic rebel" (LVM III, 2). People bore responsibility not only for their private lives and personal happiness—not to mention their constant concern for the "salvation of their souls"—but for their fellow human beings as well, for their environment and the universe.

Light and air naturally sent their greening power (*viriditas*) to germinate the seeds and in this way keep everything in the world alive for the benefit of humanity. Light and air were actually sources of nourishment.

Of equal importance for leading a healthy life was the cultivation of crops for food, in the literal sense of the German term *Lebensmittel* which combines the word for "life" (*Leben*) with the word for "means" (*Mittel*), i.e., that which is taken into the system to maintain life and growth. Eating and drinking played a decisive role in Hildegard's work, so much so that she compared the stomach to a receptacle through which all the elements of the cosmos passed in the form of food that was received, digested and expelled (LDO IV, 71). Clearly, she was referring to people's ability to comprehend the world (*capacitatem mundi ostendit*). In the act of eating, humanity daily entered into a physical relationship with all creatures (LDO IV, 105). This was why Hildegard called the stomach, the organ that she regarded as the center for digesting the elements of the world, *capax mundi*. The stomach, after all, "claims the powers of the creatures it absorbs and then expels so that it can derive nourishment from their juices. God has decreed this to be the way of nature. For there are concealed in all nature—in the animals, birds and fishes as well as in the plants, flowers and trees—certain hidden mysteries of God (*occulta mysteria Dei*) which no human being and no other creature can know or feel unless this is granted by God." (LDO IV, 105)

Measure and moderation were crucial factors in nutrition. The intake of food always had to be properly regulated. Hildegard was well aware that food often did not agree with people possessed of a sickly constitution. Therefore she advised melancholy people to eat heartily while she counseled those who were extremely jovial in temperament to moderate their diet. She did not recommend excessive fasting, because she felt that the body could not adequately replace the nourishment that had been lost. Fruit picked from the tree, for instance, was not to be stewed but peeled (PL 1060 B).

Among the various beverages, wine had a special role to play because it expressed the power of nature and the spirit. Hildegard traced viticulture back to Noah: "From that time forward the earth, sullied by the blood of Abel, brought forth the new juice of the vine, and wisdom (*sapientia*) again became effective." (PL 255 A/B) Despite any misuse "as a result of which people's carnal desires are brought to light" (PL 236 B), the natural power of wine and its great mystery were preserved. "Grain for spirits and grapes for wine will grow because of that mysterious greening power (*occulta viriditas*) that people are incapable of seeing." (PL 232 A) So far as nutrition was concerned, the seasons and the periods of the day, a person's age and productivity, and of course the state of a person's emotions all had to be taken into account. With regard to eating and drinking, what mattered most was that they be regulated (*regulariter*) and carried out in a social setting (*communiter*) (PL 1060 D). Everything that happened during the course of a year, over a lifetime, or in a day was governed by a definite rhythm. The same applied to the interaction between movement and rest (*motus et quies*) reflecting the relation between prayer and work (*ora et labora*). Everything was part of the grand scheme of time, embedded in temporal reality, in a monastic regimen aptly summarized in an inscription on the headstone of a Benedictine abbot: Arrange your time in the times allotted (*tempora tempore tempera*).

In his report on monastic life in the convent at Rupertsberg, Guibert of Gembloux wrote: "Everything here exudes a spirit of devotion, holiness, and tranquillity. On Sundays the looms, spindles, and pens rest. The nuns listen in rapt silence to devotional readings and liturgical songs." On workdays, "they follow the words of the apostle: If anyone will not work, let him not eat. In their workrooms (*officinae*) they toil zealously to copy books, weave garments and perform other kinds of manual labor (*opera manuum*) and on account of their avid reading the light of divine knowledge (*illuminatio divinae cognitionis*) and the grace of remorse (*gratia compunctionis*) flow toward them; meanwhile the performance of outside work (*exercitium*) banishes indolence, the enemy of the soul, and keeps down the garrulousness (*scurrilitas*) that can so easily become rank gossip in the mouths of those who spend time together in idleness." (P406)

Driven by a "concern for earthly things" (*cura terrenorum*), many people resembled those erring spirits "who rush everywhere." They constantly broke out in sweat and suffered from restlessness of body and soul, even though they "seek delight in this restlessness as if it were the height of quietness." (LVM IV, 42) Activity per se, however, ultimately led to ruin!

"So long as you have the opportunity," Hildegard wrote to an abbess at

Elostat, "get down to work and do your duty," for work was tantamount to calling God, to a plea! But then she continued: "Only those who plow with moderation (*per discretionem*) the field that is their body will not be devastated when death suddenly overtakes them, for the music of the Holy Spirit (*symphonia Spiritus Sancti*) and a life filled with joy (*laeta vita*) await them. Yet one must be careful not to destroy one's body by working too hard. Always remember that you cannot create another human being. Therefore ask God gently to provide you with a better life. This is more agreeable to God than inundating him in a torrent of tears and pleas." May God, Hildegard concluded, make you "a temple of life." (PL 214 C/D)

The next theme in the commentary was devoted to the wholesome cycle of wakefulness and sleep that determined our diurnal rhythm. It was no accident that day-to-day human life, with its cycle of work and leisure, was part of the grand cosmic design to divide every twenty-four period into a regular pattern of days and nights. "Although the day outshines the night, the night expresses wisdom." The night was pregnant with plans and was an extension of the day (P 554/55). The day and the night conversed and corresponded, as it were, with each other; they passed on their powers to each other and were accountable and responsible to each other. This was only understood by human beings, who knew and appreciated the change of seasons (*tempora temporum*), especially since they were kept alive and active as a result of all these things.

The sun and moon ensured the continuance of these cosmic cycles. The moon, in a sense, suckled the seasons, "just as a mother nourishes her child, first with milk and later with more substantial food" (*primo lacte, postea cibo*). And the sun shone over the earth by day, "just as we remain awake with open eyes during the daytime. But at night the sun goes under the earth, just as we sleep at night with closed eyes." (LDO IV, 99) Well-ordered wakefulness (*vigilia*) produced health (*sanitatem inferunt*); whereas too much or too little sleep damaged the nervous system and thus the entire body (PL 1056 B/C). In a living situation in which things could often become quite chaotic, one of the most important general rules was devoted to the strict regulation of the hours of the day (Ch 48.2 of the Rule). Through the association of rituals with specified periods of time, one acquired an opportunity to become better acquainted with the realities of life.

A good night's sleep was accompanied by the kinds of invigorating dreams that were formerly (*genitura mystica*) the handmaidens of prophecy but now served simply to refresh our bodies (*recreatio*). When we dreamed, the soul, like "the moon when the body sleeps," was always on the lookout; it let "its eyes wander" and saw the most wondrous things as it did. "When one awakens in a properly balanced state, one's mind is sharp, one's expression cheerful, and one can get on with one's life. All one's limbs are in perfect equilibrium."

The idea of regulating the hours of the day and night was never meant to inconvenience people. On the contrary, this salutary arrangement of time was prescribed to enhance their happiness (PL 1057 A: *Et pro recto disposito temperamento non gravabantur, sed gaudebant*).

All these natural and seemingly prosaic life processes represented an incentive for the alert human being to engage in a permanent dialogue with its creator: "In the fullness of its power the soul enters the sleeping body, awakening it and sensing through various modes of experience the one and only God."

The following point about cultivating a proper lifestyle deals with a person's own body, his or her personal hygiene, and all the mysterious metabolic processes that take place within the human organism.

Personal hygiene played a major role in the work of this astonishing medieval woman. She omitted nothing—from hair care to dental hygiene, from bathing to cosmetics. In every case her goal was "to clean and groom ourselves so that we remain beautiful!" Literally everything in this regard was taken into account: the "moistness of saliva," for instance, which like a good salve fostered the power to see, hear, smell, and speak; sneezing, blowing one's nose, sweating; "purgatives" to cleanse one's bowels (laxatives) or stomach (emetics) or veins (bloodletting); every imaginable excretion and secretion (*excreta et secreta*) in the body, not to mention the hormones and our sex lives.

All these mysterious metabolic processes pointed to the existence of a universal exchange mechanism that affected both humanity and the world in equal measure. The seas and rivers, for example, were part of such a system (LDO IV, 59). Just as water came to the surface through subterranean passages, food was evacuated after passing through the bloodstream. "Food and drink build up the blood to a juice and send it up just as yeast does to the entire loaf of dough. And so the juices remain within the body, work within it and are consumed in the process. What cannot be used from the consumed foods and drinks descends into a person's lower intestines (*inferiora*) and changes itself into excrement. When it has been transformed into excrement, it is evacuated by the body." Hildegard attached great importance to regulating digestion and used a nice image to describe the process: "It is as when grapes are pressed, the wine bottled, and what remains—that is the vines and stems—is thrown out" (CC 112).

People were supposed to follow the path of moderation throughout their personal lives. As Hildegard wrote to an abbot at Michaelsberg near Bamberg: "For God created heaven and earth in all their magnificence and combined hardship with joy (*suavia ac dura*), so that people could overcome their problems." (P 551)

The sixth and final theme in the commentary concerned the way in which people dealt, in an informed way, with their passions. It recapitulated the rules for conducting life and ended by "pulling out all the stops." In controlling the passions, we obtained a new lease on life. "Then human hearts will open to true happiness, just as flowers open in the sunshine." All the organs joyously embraced life, the *vita laeta*. And true joy grew from the passions!

In regulating our still powerful emotions, it was not "psychological" control that was called for but rather specific ways of dealing with our physical needs. Hildegard would never have spoken of "mental health" or used a namby-pamby term such as "psychosomatic"—body and soul were simply too bound up together in our emotional lives for that. Hence it was in keeping with the measure of humanity that "the movement of the rational soul (*motus rationalis animae*) and the work of the body (*opus corporis*), together with the five senses that helped make up the whole human being (*quod totus homo est*), were on a par (*parem modum*). For the soul cannot urge the body to do more than it can achieve, and the body cannot achieve more than the soul has set into motion, just as the various senses cannot be separated from one another. Rather, they cling to one another and illuminate our entire person (*totum hominem*) beneficially in both our upper and lower aspects." (LDO IV, 22)

However it was not always easy for a person to maintain self-control; one was often at the mercy of one's emotions. Did we not realize or learn every day the extent to which our likes and dislikes formed the backdrop of all our personal encounters and experiences? We were motivated by unconscious desires—more than we knew or wished to know. Therefore we needed countervailing forces and safeguards, among which joy occupied pride of place. Joy (*in gaudio et sine taedio*) was the most vital of life's elements (PL 1058 B).

Music, which Hildegard viewed as a kind of regulator, a therapeutic agent of the first order, was an especially important factor in directing a person's inner life. "For every element has its own sound, a pristine sound in God's created order, and all the tones blend into one universal harmony." In our earthly existence, of course, this magnificent celestial concert no longer embraced the primal harmonies; people were no longer in consonance with the music of the spheres (*musica mundana*), although even now every song reminded them of the nature of the celestial harmonies and of the fact that through their *musica humana* they were once in unison with all other creatures.

In spite of the finite nature of human life, people's thoughts were nevertheless directed toward the end of life, because only at the end would people—intact in body and in gender (*in integritate membrorum et cum sexu*)—reach their final salvation. By turning toward God (*conversio*) and away from sin (*poenitentia*) human beings were preparing themselves for eternal beatitude (*restitutio*), so that they could return, like the Prodigal Son, to live in harmony with the choirs of angels and their angelic hymns (*carmen angelicum*).

What we find most fascinating in Hildegard's "study of life" is the fact that, on the one hand, she included the cosmological dimensions in the conduct of human life and on the other that she was so intensely concerned with the ultimate purpose of the world (eschatology). She believed that life and death, disease and suffering—all people's crises, hardships and problems—could be comprehended only from a cosmic perspective, that everything naturally tended toward transcendence, and that all things strove for salvation!

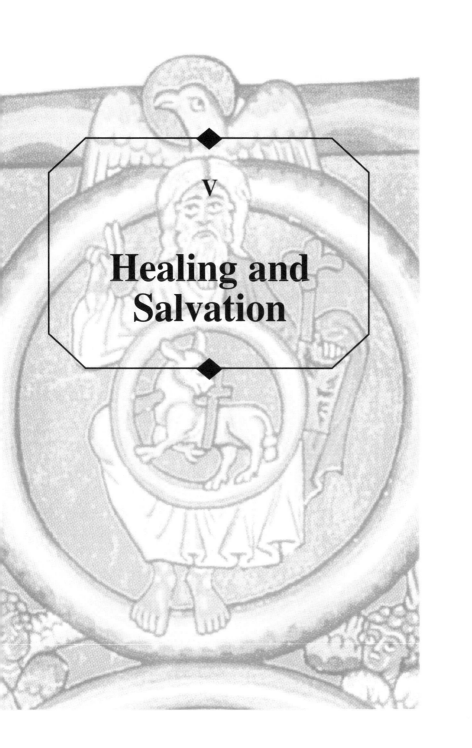

V

Healing and Salvation

1. THE WAYS OF CREATION

God's Word was at work in the world, and the construction of this world—nature around us and nature within us—had an impact in some mysterious way upon the course of events that took place within it, namely, our history. Human beings, the *opus Dei,* experienced both spheres of nature in the real world as their own reality; they grew by helping nature grow (*opus alterum per alterum*). Because of their work upon creation (*opus cum creatura*), they had a responsibility for both spheres. People were, after all, creatures of God and by nature builders of creation (Sc III, 2: *operans factum opus in operatione*).

As God's privileged creature (*opus operationis Dei*), humankind from its inception had a superior constitution and therefore a special obligation to the world. Humanity unfolded, as it were, the potentialities of the cosmos. As the creative beings par excellence (*homo operans*) people were destined to represent the created order and—as mirrors of the cosmos (*speculum universi*)—to carry out their responsibilities to nature. As the only creatures endowed with reason (*homo rationalis*) they found themselves in a uniquely creative partnership with nature. And as the creatures that were answerable for everything (*homo responsurus*) they bore full responsibility for all the purposes of creation.

Because of their transgressions human beings had also become the most fragile creatures (*homo destitutus*). Their desire to be autonomous had disturbed the tranquillity of nature; they had become "humanity the rebel" (*homo rebellis*), forced to live with their inner conflicts throughout history. Disease was merely the outward sign of this flaw, a flaw that the greening power (*viriditas*) of nature, in its turn, sought to counteract. In spite of all their inadequacies human beings focused on the end of life, so that in the end they could achieve salvation fully restored in their bodily integrity (*homo restitutus*). The Prodigal Son would be returned to the "feast of angels" and accepted into the angelic choirs (*carmen angelicum*). Henceforth we will interpret the purposes of creation from this eschatological perspective.

To illustrate the destiny of humanity—debased, alienated and impoverished—Hildegard presented us with one of her favorite parables: the parable of the Dishonest Steward. Disgraced and dismissed from office, this once talented and rich estate manager became the quintessentially flawed human being. The steward made a pact with the world (*opus cum creatura*) to redeem himself and thereby escape his alienated existence and return home to assume a new stewardship. More clever than the "children of light"—angels hardened by their malevolence—humanity would win friends by engaging in honest cultural work. Hildegard compared bringing home the cosmos—in partnership with nature—to leading a bride to the altar, to finding oneself through a cosmic reunion with the Creator and creation—with a "nature that was golden" (*materia aurea*) in a transformed universe.

Until then, however, time would be regulated and goal-oriented; it would be "God in history" and it would be directed toward God. In the midst of this drama of salvation, this "season of seasons" (*tempus temporum*) the Church (*ecclesia*) appeared at the center of Hildegard's cosmology. It was the mother of all things (*materia omnium rerum*) and the precursor of the celestial Jerusalem. A pilgrim through history, the Church informed us about our origins and provided us with insights into our present situation, along with hope for our ultimate salvation. Time thus acquired a completely new dimension.

Hildegard combined two basic symbols—"the way" (*via*) and "the wheel" (*rota*)—to form a single and surprising unity, which stood for both self-contained fulfillment and continuous development. Everything in Hildegard's dynamic cosmology was, as it were, "on the move": nature, the seasons, and humanity who while in transit, on the way, inside the revolving wheel of time, made the responsible decision to pursue a definite goal, the cosmic Christ, which meant, above all *Sci vias Domini*, "Know the ways of God!"

God not only guided his creatures to the light, he multiplied them

(LVM I, 47). From the germinating power of the developing cosmos, he brought the world to full maturity (*prosperitas egregiendi*) and complete perfection (LVM III, 28: *ad completionem perfectionis*) within a process of perpetual flux (*transmutatio indeficiens*). God's Word glowed in the human figure (*clarescit in forma hominis*), and humankind was reflected in the Word (*et ideo fulgemus in illo*). Humanity helped to build the limbs of God's beautiful body (P 457/58: *aedificantes membra sui pulchri corporis*).

Thus God created human beings and gave them the whole world so that they could work with nature, that part of the created order which, in accord with its essence, always dwelt within and yet transcended every human being. Only humanity was conscious of this inner meaning of reality. God had, after all, endowed people with the attribute of intelligence (*rationabilis vita*) and by doing so made them like the angels (*in una rationalitate conjuncta*). Only in this sense can humanity (*homo rationalis*) be regarded as a rational being (*rationalis vita*), one that dared to make decisions and take responsibility.

The foundational human ability—reason—had the power to discern all things (*rationalitas discernit omnia*). It investigated and explored all creatures; it analyzed and studied them (*omnia subtiliter penetrat et discutit*). It was because of this intellectual faculty that God allowed humanity to turn like a wheel, in the spirit of life (*in spiritu vitae circuire*). God left people to their own devices and then called them back home, while keeping the whole world in his hands and working upon everything in the cosmos (*Deus omnia comprehendit, quoniam omnia operatus est*).

Hildegard returned to the Dishonest Steward, but this time in the person of Adam who symbolized for her the loss of paradise and the consequent history of salvation, which in its turn was connected surprisingly to the fate of man and woman together. "Since God quickly asked, 'Adam, where are you?' this indicated that he who had created people in the divine image and likeness wished to draw them back to himself." Hildegard immediately shifted the image to the fate of the first couple who were to be in agreement with each other, like the body and soul God had joined together in unity (LDO I, 15). Both man and woman were directly and personally addressed by the One, bound by an oath of loyalty and in search of salvation.

Time and again Hildegard referred to the dialogue between the Creator and his creatures which God conducted in a spirit of harmony, or better, in the way that lovers do. God had, after all, favored humanity with the gift of his great love. "The creatures' obedience to God in all things showed how they wanted to kiss the Creator." (LVM V, 39) God created humanity to strive for salvation and perfection. In accord with their nature, people shared in the work of perfecting creation; they became, as it were, partners in the divine revelation, in the ways of creation that led to salvation.

On the road to salvation all human virtues (*virtutes*) came as endowments from God, "the Head of all true joy" (Sc III, 9), and worked together for the maturation of the human soul, a process fostered by what Hildegard praised in the Holy Spirit as "the innermost life force of nature" (*vita vitae creaturae*), the "firebrand of love," the sole purpose of which was salvation.

One last time Hildegard presented us with Adam, "the begetter of the entire human race" who pointed the way to the Son of God "who was made flesh in the body of a virgin" and produced "spiritual people." "They shall be fecund, just as by means of an angel God promised Abraham that his seed would be as numerous as the stars of heaven." (LDO I, 16)

From among this astral offspring, God—as Hildegard suggestively concluded in her first book of cosmology—chose the "dormant earth" (*terra dormiens*), in other words, the Virgin Mary, the new Eve, the grand symbol—woman as the symbol of divine reality! In her great humility she was the king's enclosed bridal chamber (*clausus cubiculus regis*). God himself wished to dwell within her secret womb. And since God promised Abraham that his progeny would be "as numerous as the stars of heaven," he foresaw that one day Abraham's offspring would complete "the fullness of the heavenly community" (*plenus numerus caelestis consortii*) (LDO I, 17).

2. HUMANKIND AS RESPONSIBLE CREATURE

With the creative completion of this process of ordering the cosmos, people acquired a locus for their activities and a place from which to orient themselves. Hildegard's guidelines for a well-ordered world, on the other hand, appeared in the form of the virtues (*virtutes*) which together with virility (*virilitas*) and verdant power (*viriditas*) formed an alliterative trio.

Given a cosmology such as Hildegard's, it was only natural that the virtues found a place in her concept of natural history and the healing arts, for they had a physiological basis and a therapeutic function, not to mention being perfect models for a society bereft of ideas and ideals. The virtues demonstrated what it meant to take a stand and assume responsibility in any given situation. In sum, they were humanity's crowning achievement (*perficitur*), "for they are brought about in people by God" (*opus operantis hominis in Deo*) (Sc III, 3).

Discretion (*prudentia*)—which Hildegard called "the mother of virtues"—occupied pride of place. With the foreknowledge (*pro-videntia*) of discretion God ordered the structure of the cosmos and paved the way for the unfolding of history. This was the world in which people lived and worked as rational beings (*homo rationalis*); all other creatures were mute (*creatura muta*), lacking the power of articulate speech. People did not truly come alive until they soared on the wings of reason (*in pennis rationalitatis vitalis est*) and it was only through reason that they were able to lavish care and attention on living things with the prudence that blossomed forth from Discretion (*prosperitas prudentiae*). In this scheme of things, God also endowed the heart with reason (*cor rationalitatem habet*). The intellect—a unique kind of spirituality—flourished in sex as well (*et in lumbis rationalitas floret*). In all spheres of life, to act with discretion was to act rationally, that is, to take cognizance of reality, to let it come through, to be reasonable and open, to take the measure of things and then take the proper measures, to enjoy the taste of things as they really were. Only thus were human beings (*homo sapiens*) capable of directing itself and others with discretion.

In order to govern themselves and others, however, people needed another virtue—justice (*justitia*). By its very nature, the idea of justice tended in the direction of social order; it was a virtue practiced toward the other person, toward one's neighbor. Justice meant leaving each person his or her own space and respecting the other person. Every being in the world had to show consideration for all other beings. Human beings had their existence at the crossroads of worldly concerns (*in quadruvio saecularium curarum*) (LDO II, 16). Hildegard extolled justice as the fruit that grew from balancing different forces, and again using refreshingly graphic language she described the liver, the great center of metabolism, as the citadel of justice (*fortitudo justitiae*). Justice therefore had no less a task than fitting a human being into his or her social environment and at the same time allowing all other human beings to be themselves, according them what was rightfully theirs, showing concern for them, and doing this day after day in the everyday world of concrete reality that, in fact, was made up wholly of interpersonal relationships.

It was also within a purely social nexus that we encounter fortitude (*fortitudo*), which time and again dared to challenge evil with courage and coolness. Advised by discretion, fortitude was the first virtue to acquire its inner form and thus its particular standing. In the case of the virtues it was of paramount importance that they be balanced, for if one believed oneself to be resting on justice and brimming over with scruples, one would merely be preparing for the "pitfall of weariness" (*laqueus fatigationis*) because one had abandoned "gentleness of spirit" and "prudence of foresight." Finally, one might doubt one's own courage and fall into the "snare of despair" (*laqueus desperationis*) and try to manage without any virtues at all (LDO III, 14).

Finally, Hildegard presented us with what she regarded, in the vicissitudes of time, as the authoritative criterion for moderation (*temperantia*), namely, discretion (*discretio*). Discretion was for her the root (*radix prima*) of every action; it constituted, as it were, the firmament of life. "Below it is the earth which stands for the *vita activa*, and above it is heaven, the *vita contemplativa*." Thus discretion performed its healing function with moderation and self-restraint and tempered all things (*discretio temperat omnia*).

This was why *Discretio* answered the vice of immoderation as follows: "All the things that are in God's plan reciprocate each other's actions (*sibi invicem responsum dant*). The stars twinkle from the light of the moon, and the moon glows from the fire of the sun. All things are subordinate to greater things and do not surpass them . . . And so I walk in the light of the moon and sun, and I think about God's plan. I rise up with all these things in honesty. I enumerate them with great charity, for I am a leader (*princeps*) in the palace of the King, and I know all his secrets. I leave nothing out; rather, I bring everything together. And I am very fond of all these things." (LVM II, 22)

Hildegard used another, surprisingly simple image to orient humanity in the world. She returned to the four elements, linking them to their corresponding virtues. First there was *earth* that contained the seeds of all things that germinated and the greening power that brought forth all the flowers. The earth constituted, as it were, the flower and glory of God's manly strength, for his virility was adorned with all the things of the earth. The earth exalted the potency of this *Vir Deus*, for it was the earth that supplied the material with which God worked upon humanity and from which he made his Son human (LVM IV, 29).

Every creature was both root and seed and brought forth fruit, becoming bread and wine and part of the cosmic banquet. Similarly, the holy ones were purified in the *fire* of the Holy Spirit. This Fire Spirit gave out all good things, stirred up all good things, and kindled all good things. This was the foundation upon which God built holiness up high in the *air*. Greening power's gentle breath of life increased the craving for the food of life.

Finally, the Holy Spirit, using *water* with its many powers, sent forth comforting warmth, dissolved the coagulation of sins, caused all things to flow toward spiritual things in the flood of truth, turned even brittle legal precepts to liquid, and "through the greenness of the innermost sighs of humanity, he pours the moisture of remorse on their hardened hearts." Humankind ascended into the air like the birds, swam in the waters of faith like a fish, went out to pasture like the animals of the field, crept in the footsteps of humility like a reptile—and like all other creatures was always headed toward greater sanctity (LVM VI, 20–23).

At the end of time humankind would resemble the golden rim of a wheel (*aureus circulus rotae*), and with them all of nature would become part of a cycle of perpetual transmutation (*transmutatio indeficiens*). God had perfected his work in humanity (*omnia opera sua perfecit*).

In this spiritual setting humanity proved to be a completely responsible being. Therefore Hildegard stated at the end of her principal work on ethics that God, "the builder of the cosmos" (*fabricator mundi*), had given people the opportunity to do their own work (*opera sua*) using their God-given knowledge and the elements that the Creator had put at their disposal. "Therefore human beings should not let any other creature dictate their work. Rather, they should bring their work to completion by themselves (*per semetipsum*)." (LVM VI, 59) God had endowed people with an astonishing degree of autonomy, as a result of which they were confronted with the necessity of making decisions in every situation. This decision-making was a continual process of balancing one good against another. It was the product of an existential attitude and had to be started from scratch every time a new situation arose.

According to Hildegard, it was God's will that human beings should have the freedom to decide. She spoke in this context of the "wheel of knowledge" (*rota scientiae*) which showed us only in which direction to turn (LVM III, 27). With the power to make decisions people possessed "a living treasure," and with the faculty of reason (*vis rationalitatis*) they could begin their work. Man was part of a fascinating network of interrelationships that involved claims and obligations, empathy and communication, compliance and decision.

Freedom was an integral part of human nature. In "knowledgeable love" (*in scientia caritatis*) God led his likeness, body and soul (*anima et corpore*), to the "fullness of salvation" (*ad plenitudinem integrationis*) (LDO I, 11). God, however, did not abandon people to their freedom; he took them under his protection, just as a hen gathered her young under her wing. "For God did not want to have his glory alone, so he distributed it among his creatures so that they could rejoice in it with him." (LVM I, 136) Therefore Wisdom (*sapientia*), referred to here as "God's eye," was often shown giving the gift of knowledge in freedom. God embraced wisdom, his "dearest friend," in ardent love as she stood before him. Despite all his planning, God sought the counsel of wisdom; when human beings in their freedom availed themselves of her help, they were called "the pinnacle of heaven"!

This particular arrangement of the virtues as a way to orient humanity in the world was based on the profound physiological insight that it was always the same fundamental forces and needs that were capable of either preserving or destroying our basic inner needs. Despite all the splendid parables, it was nature at its most basic level that sought to force itself into our field of vision, with the hope of being cultivated in a humane manner. Humanity's task was to work with and upon the world (*opus cum creatura*), to produce a world order that could also serve as a model for the way of nature. The virtues were the means of attaining that self-realization that was continually striving for God (*opus operantis hominis in Deo*).

3. ORIENTING HUMANITY IN THE WORLD

The interplay of the virtues and vices, which Hildegard presented to us so dramatically in her *Liber Vitae Meritorum*, helped her to orient humanity in the world. She set the virtues against the vices in a kind of verbal combat, where the job of the virtues was to answer the words of the vices and thereby overcome them. At the beginning of the first major vision there appeared the imposing figure of a man whom Hildegard introduced as *Vir Deus*. This man was God, and Hildegard referred specifically to the verse in the Old Testament (Isaiah 42:13) where God was the man of whom the prophet said: "The Lord shall go forth as a mighty man." In Hildegard's vision, however, a fiery cloud, in which a fiery crowd lived, emerged from the mouth of the "Man-God." This cloud contained the vices (*vitia*) which she subsequently arrayed against the virtues (*virtutes*) in a series of dramatic interactions.

The man's feet stood in the waters of the abyss, and he towered above the earth, his face shining with brightness in the serene ether. However the imposing figure did not remain still; it began to turn, and as it turned, the destiny of the cosmos unfolded (LVM I, 3). It was clearly no accident that Hildegard correlated the proportions of the man's body with the spheres of the universe, and that she compared the tragic history of humankind to the dramatic stages of salvational history. The elements of the material world encountered the universe of time, for it was the spiritual virtues (*virtutes*) that mediated between the ether and the abyss, between body and soul, and between God and his people. God's will and the final judgment were part of a cycle, and between them stood humanity, the responsible being.

In this way Hildegard illuminated the *Theatrum mundi* and set the stage for the drama. In a bizarre and awesome display, she arrayed antithetical pairs of thirty-five sins set against thirty-five virtues. In a series of verbal combats, the virtues answered the words of the vices. In this battle over the moral destiny of humankind, it was the diabolical power of the "ancient serpent," filled with venom and vitriol, that was first loosed upon that fragile creature called humankind. Its arguments seemed quite reasonable on the surface, though they were at the same time filled with mockery: "All those who call themselves the sun through works of light, I shall make them repulsive and benighted and horrible in darkness!" And then with a monstrous rumble it screamed: "No one should adore another God who does not see and know him. What kind of a God would it be whom people worshipped but had never seen!"

Hildegard deliberately confronted the problem of theodicy, namely, how could God in his omnipotence and omniscience at the same time be loving and kind? How could a God of love, all-knowing and all-powerful, permit the existence of natural and moral evil? And if God were in fact Providence, why in his omnipotence could he not have discovered a different way to salvation, one without all these tragic detours? Hildegard asked tersely: "If God wished me to be just and good, why did he not make me virtuous (Sc I, 4: *Si Deo placet ut justus et bonus sim, quare non facit me rectum*)?" However, since our destiny reposed in the eye of God—even though God had concealed the ultimate reason for creation from us (Sc I, 2)—Hildegard again brought the problem of theodicy back to human beings, who had to make decisions in the real world but were not entitled to base those decisions on their ultimate place in that world!

The first figure to make its appearance was Worldly Love. It looked like a black person who was naked. It had its arms and legs wrapped around a tree, reached for the flowers on the tree and picked them playfully, saying: "I hold all the world's kingdoms with their bountiful greatness in my hands. Why should I wither when I have all this greenness in my hands? Since I am young, why should I shuffle about like an old person? Why should I lose my sight to blindness? I will hang onto the beauty of this world blissfully and enjoy it so long as I can! I do not understand all these words spoken about another life, a better world, when I have never seen it!" (LVM I, 10)

Thus spoke Worldly Love, but no sooner had it finished speaking than the root of the tree dried up and the tree fell into darkness, pulling the eerie image into the darkness with it. Immediately the voice of Heavenly

Love was heard in answer to the words of the first image: "You are fool-ish thinking that you possess all of life with only a spark from the ashes! What do you know about a life where the beauty of youth (*in pulchritu-dine juventutis*) lasts forever and where old age never comes . . . You live from moment to moment and dry up like hay. You have fallen into the lake of destruction. I, however, am the pillar of heavenly harmony. I provide all the joys in life. Life is what I care about!" (LVM I, 11)

The verbal sparring between the other virtues and vices continued in a similar manner: "What kind of person thinks only of dying? An empty person! So let us be happy while we can be!" (LVM I, 12) Thus spoke Impudence, followed immediately by Jesting (*joculatrix*): "Why should I be mournful and mope! We are entitled to have fun and play. I will be playful in many different ways and let my happy heart rejoice in the beauty of nature. And why shouldn't I? Fun and games rule the world, and this is appropriate!" (LVM I, 14)

The vulgar voice of the common herd came through clearly in the words of Cowardice: "I will do nothing to risk my life by exerting myself on someone else's behalf. Mad as things are in this world, I will remain quiet. It is better to run away from the strong than to fight them. I chose my own house and need nothing more. If I fight with someone, I might just start something I could not finish." (LVM I, 19) It is easy to envision Foolish Joy spewing out its thoughtless turns of phrase: "I live a sweet life. It is nice to indulge in pleasure. Why shouldn't I? God gave us this life to take pleasure in our flesh! I know life and I want to live it to the fullest." (LVM I, 25)

These various personality types are clearly recognizable from our own daily lives—now and in the past, not to mention the future! We have all come across people who are on an ego trip and feel as though they would be utter fools not to enjoy all the beautiful things of this world. There are other people who would walk over corpses to get what they want. They seek total control, as would anyone who was not a complete fool—or so they think. They will do whatever is for their own good and would never dance to anyone else's tune (LVM II, 9). Why hold anything back from oneself and reap no reward! If you had to live in such a way that you couldn't breathe, what would life be worth? Everybody should live in accord with his or her own nature (LVM II, 21)! And if the nature of flesh had really been that troublesome to God, He could have made it more difficult to satisfy the demands of the flesh: "Heaven, therefore, has its own justice and earth seeks its own favors." (LVM III, 22) Still others do not know any other life than that they see and touch. They seek no other reality and forgo all knowledge of it. And even if they asked the sun and moon what they ought to do, they would not get an answer. They only know what they see (LVM III, 16)!

The primal sin for which God expelled Adam from paradise was Pride (*superbia*). To Hildegard it was the cause and source (*materia et matrix*) of all the misery in the world. The image of Pride spoke: "My voice cries aloud beyond the mountains. Who can match me? I spread my mantle over the hills and valleys, and I do not want anyone to fight against me. I know that I am without equal!" (LVM III, 5) Humility responded courageously. While flesh was raising up its hill of Pride, the soul in building up Humility was pressuring humanity to stop roaming about on the paths of vanity. As dams protected valleys from downpours, Humility guarded people against evil, for the essence of the soul was Humility (LDO IV, 80). Humility became a role model of the first order because its powerful shield (*scutum fortissimum*) warded off all the evil in the world. Hildegard acclaimed it a regal virtue (*regina virtutum*), a remedy (*medicina vera*), a healing substance (*medicamen*).

In the figure of youthful Aimlessness Hildegard gave us a particularly modern image whose wanderings (*vagatio*) were depicted as follows: "It would be foolish of me to remain in one place and always associate with the same people. On the contrary, I want to show myself everywhere. I want to have my voice heard everywhere. Only in this way will my glory spread. Grass grows and blossoms appear: if this were not the case with human beings too, what glory could he expect? I am like the grass with my power of reason and wisdom, and I am like a blossom with my beauty; therefore, I appear everywhere." (LVM V, 6)

Constancy (*stabilitas*) responded as follows to this profligate attitude and its demand to stand out: "As grass turns to hay, you and your cunning will wither away and you will be trampled under foot like the dirt of the road. You do not sift through the words of reason but instead jump around like locusts. You will be scattered about like snow. You have not eaten the food of wisdom or drunk the drink of moderation (*discretio*). You live like birds who have no nests. You are like ashes and rotting things. Therefore you will never find rest." (LVM V, 7)

Hildegard later interpreted the image of Aimlessness in a more systematic manner and incorporated it in her eschatology: "Such a person gads about like a vagabond taking everything that was disposed correctly into immoderation. His image has a youthful form because it does not reflect upon heaven with joy or earth with care, and he sees aimlessness in everything. He provides nothing correctly and divides nothing correctly. He does all of his work with a juvenile lack of concern." The outward image was meant to inspire admiration and veneration; the inner being was bored and weary. These people were either bursting with enthusiasm or merely lukewarm. In general, they were like oversalted food. Trapped in the web of their own will, they lacked confidence. They constantly sought new diversions, yet they wanted quiet stability. They began nothing correctly and completed nothing correctly, and with their ambivalent attitude they rushed like restless clouds. "They are looking everywhere, and always erring everywhere. They are looking for things they do not know and seeking strange places in which to dwell." (LVM V, 38)

Once again Stability (*stabilitas*) addressed Aimlessness. She noted that a truly "honest man who strives devoutly for veneration and stability" should speak to Christ in the words of the Scripture (Song of Songs 1:7): "Tell me, you whom my heart loves, where you pasture your flock, where you give them rest at midday, lest I be found wandering after the flocks of your companions." This, according to Hildegard's rather lengthy commentary, meant the following: "Wisdom said these things through Solomon, for having been immersed in wisdom, he spoke to Wisdom with the intimacy of love, as though to a woman. And Wisdom (*sapientia*) said: 'I then rose up and shook my mantle off and drenched it with a hundred thousand drops of precious dew, for in this gift God shows that he values humanity. Thus we spoke in turn. For as I ordered all things when I surrounded the circle of heaven, I also spoke through Solomon, with the love of the Creator for the creature and the creature for the Creator. I spoke about how the Creator bestowed his great love on the creature, and how the creature was obedient to him in the fervent hope of being kissed by the Creator. And when the creature was kissed by the Creator, God gave it all the things it needed.

'I, however, compare the great love of the Creator for the creature and the creature for the Creator to the love and faith by which God joins a man and woman together so that they can have children. As every creature proceeded from God, so also every creature looks back obligingly to God and does not do anything without God's instruction, just as a woman looks to her husband so that she can fulfill his commands in a way that is pleasing to him. Similarly, the creature is drawn to the Creator when it is submissive to him in all things, and the Creator is present to the creature when he gives it greenness and strength. The whole of creation would be made black if it did not use its talent correctly, but it is beautiful when it does its duty justly. Therefore, only as the creature is submissive to the Creator is the creature's reputation enhanced and the divine order preserved, for it is the Creator who brings forth everything to satisfy the creature's needs.'" (LVM V, 39)

Therefore, Hildegard concluded, the creature could speak to the Creator as if it were speaking to its beloved. It could claim a place of quietness, a home, which God was prepared in his love to give. Humanity, however, was and remained the paragon of creation (*omnis creatura*) (LVM V, 40). God wished to kiss this his own piece of work (*officiale opus*), and out of love for human beings he put the world at their disposal (*officium omnis creaturae*).

All of creation would one day resound in jubilation (*in symphonia sonet*) and all the harps in heaven play (*caelestia organa*), their sound carried on high to the celestial harmonies (*ad caelestem harmoniam*). The angels would rejoice and sing God's praises (*in laudibus sonent*) and everything would be aglow in radiant harmony (*in caelesti harmonia fulget*).

"As people are angelic creatures through their praise of God (*laus*), they are human beings through their works (*opus*). Humankind is full of God's work (*plenum opus Dei*), and all of God's miracles are accomplished through people's praise and work." (LVM V, 96).

4. The Completion of the World

In a letter to Abbot Adam of the monastery at Ebrach in the Steiger-wald, Hildegard described how in a bright vision she had seen a beautiful girl. Every creature called this girl "sovereign lady." To Hildegard this radiant girl was introduced as "Divine Love"; her dwelling place was in eternity. Love was the matrix of creation. Out of love God dressed himself in humanity. "Divine love created people, but humility redeemed them. Hope is, as it were, the eye of divine love; celestial love its heart. Faith is, as it were, the eye of humility; obedience its heart. Divine love was in eternity, and, in the beginning of all sanctity, it brought forth all creatures." (PL 192–194) Love was at work in the circles of eternity, without reference to time, like heat within a fire. "In his divine providence God foresaw all creatures that were created in the fullness of divine love for the service of humanity, and he bound them to humanity the way a flame is bound to fire." (LDO I, 13)

Hildegard pursued this train of thought further and put it on a rational plane by having Divine Love appear as Reason (*rationalitats*). The Word (*verbum*) resounded from the source of divine love, grew louder and assumed the form of work (*opus*). Wisdom (*sapientia*) emerged from the heart of the Father and was praised as "God's confidante." Hildegard regarded the Word and Reason as one. All work was to be done through perceptible Wisdom so that we might see and hear it and experience the joy of life (*vita laeta*).

Hildegard's startling conclusion was that a life of joy was contingent on self-love (*diligens et se ipsum*). "If you love God, you love your salvation (*salutem tuam*). And, loving yourself in all this, you shall also love your neighbor (*proximum*)." (Sc III, 8) Nevertheless, God, in the Grace of his Holy Spirit, made this fragile human creature a citizen of the heavenly community by bestowing the light of Reason on it.

The heart—not the head—was the central organ of universal Reason. The heart was the gateway to the cosmos, for the heart of the cosmos was Divine Love: "Whoever grasps this will never be off the mark either as to height or breadth, for love is at the center of all things." (Sc III, 13) It is neither excessive nor rash, presumptuous nor self-absorbed, diffused nor ephemeral, for it was and continued to be the heart of all being. Thus the heart was life and the foundation of our existence (*vita et fundamentum*)." (LDO IV, 105)

So much for the spiritual setting of creation that illuminated the entire cosmos. The holy ones still had to work under the strain of their bodies. The actual situation of human beings—how they were to live until the end of their days—had yet to be considered. There were still many wondrous things in the cosmos that were hidden from humankind. "Just as no one can look into the abyss, so also no one knows what will happen after the end of time." (LVM I, 45) And in any event where would one find the person who might, as it were, get to the bottom of all this? "No one, except God, who created it." (LVM I, 46) Even the blessed in heaven still did not possess true joy, since they were separated from their mortal remains: "They cannot see the face of the Father completely. The parts of the whole cannot, after all, see the whole completely. When, however, their bodies have risen again in their wholeness (*integer*), they will look at that which is whole completely and will never be changed again." (LVM I, 42)

These ideas are characteristic of Hildegard's thinking and fundamental to her concept of anthropology. She now carried them to their logical conclusion, for on the day of judgment the holy ones would sing praises of joy to those who had been made whole. "The flesh keeps the spirit shackled within the body, but the spirit will later create its own body and, therefore, humanity will be whole and holy." (LVM IV, 50) The end of the ways of God through his sanctification of the world was corporeal existence.

Now we may begin to understand how fundamental the seemingly secular idea of the "nature of the body" was to the created order and the drama of salvation. Even the blessed, said Hildegard, "yearn for divine love" so that they might live "in greater bliss" after the restoration of their bodies (LVM V, 63). Hildegard sang in the spirit of the Song of Songs 5:1: "Eat, O friends, and drink: drink deeply, O lovers!" In other words, eat in faith from the body of the Lord, the "true medicine" (*vera medicina*); drink in hope from the wine, the "cup of salvation" (*poculum salutis*), be inebriated with love! (Sc II, 6)

In the last days of the world, "humankind will be resurrected in one moment with limbs and bodies intact, each in his or her own gender (*in integritate et corporis et sexus sui*)." (Sc III, 12) On the day of divine judgment the soul will receive its cherished mantle and dear garment, the body. It will then behold God's countenance in all its splendor along with the angels.

Figure 10. The Day of Judgment
(Cod. lat. Ms. 1 (ca 1165), Hessische Landesbibliothek Wiesbaden, *Scivias* III, 12)

"Afterward, the angels will once again be elated in their hymns of praise, just as they were on the first day of creation when the victory they won in battle illuminated them. Only after the day of judgment will the angels find fulfillment in the praises of God. They will start to sing their hymns of glory in praise of the new wonder of God's creation—humankind. From then on they will play upon the zither, a sound of great joy that never wearies, never slacks and never stops. And just as they wish constantly to behold the face of God, they will never cease to be in awe of the works God has accomplished through humanity. For humankind is a being made up of body and soul, and exists as God's work with all of creation" (LDO IV, 104: *opus Dei cum omni creatura*).

The wheel had come full circle. Love was the principle of creation and salvation as well as the prime cause (*causa principalis*) of creation and the Incarnation. In the beginning, love was the matrix of creation. We were redeemed by love, and love would bring the cosmos to completion. But love never stood alone. It grew wings and became fiery Reason (*ignea rationalitas*).

At the end of time the hymn of praise sung responsively between the Creator and the creature would begin to sound again. God directed his love toward humanity. He was counting on us! God was relying on us, and we put our trust in him. He held us in his loving embrace (*amando amplexus*) and out of sheer love he entrusted us with the fullness of creation (*officium omnis creaturae*). For love created the world, and love would make it whole again.

5. THE END OF TIME

What we viewed and marveled at as the created order at the beginning of this work in Chapter III once again appears to us in all its grandiose splendor as we turn our attention to the fate of the world. Hildegard maintained the same basic eschatological mood throughout all the boldly crafted visions that follow below, visions of the transformation of nature, the completion of history, the glorification of the body, and the construction of a "golden city" at the end of time.

The first thing Hildegard saw at the end of the world in the final vision of her theological works was the emergence of the long hoped-for age of peace: "In these days sweet clouds will touch the earth with gentle breezes and cause it to overflow with the power of greenness and fertility. Then people will focus on justice, which the world lacked in the age of womanish weakness. The princes and the people will put God's precepts into proper practice. They will forbid all weapons made to kill people and permit only tools that are needed for cultivating the fields and that are for the benefit of mankind." (LDO X, 20) They shall beat their swords into plowshares. Humankind had reached maturity and brought nature under cultivation.

At the end of time humanity would resemble the golden rim of a wheel (*aureus circulus rotae*). "Purified in spirit and in body humanity will come to full maturity, and the secrets of the deepest mysteries will be revealed to humanity." (LVM VI, 17) And with humanity all of nature would become part of a cycle of perpetual transmutation (*transmutatio indeficiens*). Humanity was the fulfillment of God's work (*omnia opera sua perfecit*).

In the concrete context of the world the Incarnation was comprehensible solely as a cosmic event. Humanity was a reflection of the cosmic Christ, for in the flesh of his Son God had assumed a human form so that he could bring humanity and the world home to the heavenly Jerusalem. The celestial homecoming would manifest itself in the end of the cosmic nexus, at which time all the elements would be purified. This would be followed by the dawning of the day of revelation. The river of time would flow into the sea of eternity. Then the world would appear in a blazing fire, "a world that will rise up from the living waters that cover its hills and mountains. And the whole world will sing angelic songs." (LVM IV, 31)

What applied to the edifice of nature and the structure of the cosmos was now directed toward the course of history. Indeed, judgment was passed on history and thus on time itself. This would become evident at the end of time, after the cosmic disaster had began and was consummated.

"After this I look, and behold, all the elements and creatures are shaken by frightful upheavals. Fire bursts forth, the air dissolves, waters over-

Figure 11. The new heaven above
the transformed Cosmos
(Cod. lat. Ms. 1 (ca 1165), Hessische
Landesbibliothek Wiesbaden, *Scivias* III, 12)

flow, and the earth begins to move. Lightning flashes, thunder crashes, the mountains open up, forests fall, and all that is mortal expires. And all the elements are purified, and all pain vanishes and is no more." (Sc III, 12)

And a voice echoed through all the world : "O ye sons of man who lie in the earth, rise! And behold, in one moment the bones of the dead, wherever they were in the world, were brought together. They were covered with flesh and rose intact in body and in gender (*in integritate membrorum et cum sexu*). And their works appeared in them openly." Suddenly from the East a brilliant light flashed: "And in a cloud I saw the Son of Man with the same face he had had on earth and with his wounds still open, coming in my direction. He was accompanied by the angelic choirs. He sat upon a throne of flame, glowing but not burning. Beneath him the great tempest that was purifying the world began to rage . . .

"When the judgment ended, the thunder and lightning, the winds and tempests ceased, the transitory parts of the elements vanished instantly. And a great calm came . . .

"Then the elements shone in all their splendor, as if a black skin had been removed from them. Fire no longer had its raging heat, air its opacity, water its turbulence, earth its instability. The sun and moon and stars sparkled in the firmament like jewels. Standing still and not moving in orbit, they no longer separated day from night. There was no night, just day. This was the end." (Sc III, 12)

At the end of time, when the cosmos was completed, we were to learn all the secrets of Heaven, but only, as it were, through a glass darkly (*fenestraliter*), as if reflected in a mirror (*quasi per speculum*). For too long life had been concealed within God's omnipotence, waiting in silence for the white cloud to shine forth. "Then the dawn rose up and embraced the sun, and the sun sent out its rays and built a great city. The sun produced twelve lights and in the reflection of holiness it awakened those who slept." (LVM IV, 31)

Thus the "golden city" was built, the city that Hildegard extolled as the "heavenly Jerusalem," radiant in the eternal light. It was built upon fallen rocks, that is, lost sheep whom the Son of God had found and made part of the foundation. The windows in the city were made out of topazes and sapphires, and the walls sparkled with living gemstones. The towers shimmered in gold and shone forth in the radiance of the blessed, for in the center of the city there appeared a cloud filled with holy ones, the elect in inner beauty resplendent in the rich greenness of ripe fruit. The Holy Spirit sang and danced within them!

The golden city was built entirely (*plena constructio*) of living stones joined together. Like a giant metropolis it took in the multitudes of all nations, just as a huge net holds a prodigious catch of fish (Sc III, 2). Then "the builders of the glorious celestial Jerusalem" would take possession of their Golden City, "resplendent in the light of eternal life." The "shining blossoms on the splendid body of the Word who was the Son of God" came home intact in body to live their lives in fullness in their heavenly home. Overflowing with the love of the celestial harmonies the blissful music of the wedding march resounded. Humanity and God formed a union again, this time forever. Love had completed the cosmic cycle!

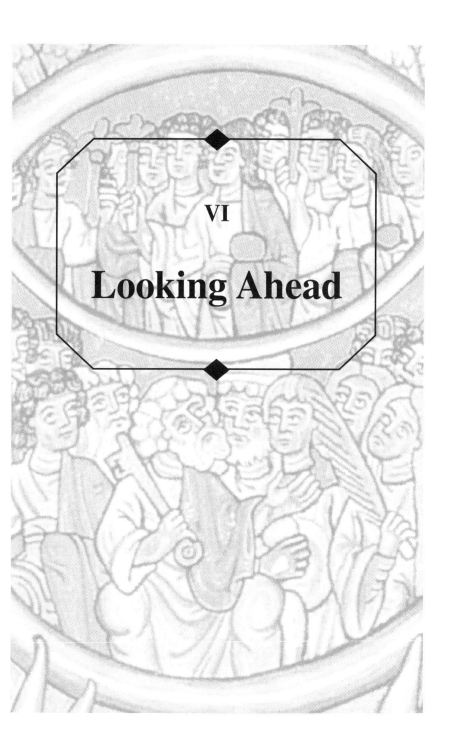

VI

Looking Ahead

As we come to the end of our fantastic journey through the world of the Middle Ages—a world outside our own experience and yet somehow familiar to us—we would like to take a look back for a moment and then look ahead. Our aim was to let the visions in Hildegard's works speak for themselves. They represent a vision of the world in the form of a world of visions that she presents to us in her own inimitable way.

What Hildegard's vision of humanity and the cosmos really means and what relevance it has for our own time cannot be reduced to a formula, it has to be brought to light layer by layer, bit by bit, step by step. Her visions are composed in the symbolic language of the High Middle Ages, a language that deserves our respect and on which we must of necessity base our interpretations. At the same time, as I have tried to show, we see reflected in that idiom the daily lives of real people. We are dealing, of course, with forms of expression used by a world in the remote past, forms with which we are no longer truly conversant and that have to be rephrased, interpreted and translated in order to be understood. And yet the anthropology that underlies Hildegard's writings is still persuasive, insightful, surprisingly familiar and comprehensible to those of us living at the end of the second millennium.

Hildegard of Bingen had no demonstrable forerunners and no successor. The church historian Ignaz von Döllinger described her as "a unique and unparalleled phenomenon in the history of Christianity."

Our study has of necessity been limited to the main points in Hildegard's work and had to omit any discussion of such major topics as the angelic choirs, the structure of the cosmos, the structure and destiny of the Synagogue and the Church, her stirring liturgical songs, and her astounding written correspondence that covered the length and breadth of Europe. We could only mention briefly such key concepts as *rationalitas*, *speculum*, *discretio*, and *viriditas* which suggest comparison with certain cosmological visions.

However even a work as concise and self-contained as this shows how inadequate our understanding of Hildegard would be if we had limited our discussion to the herbal remedies and potions of so-called "Hildegardian Medicine" or viewed her merely as an early prototype of the women's liberation movement or went so far as to let her be co-opted by any of the various cults that exist today. A collection of Hildegardian curiosities would simply obscure what is truly memorable about this great figure.

In spite of the boldness of her imagery Hildegard's ideas were more orthodox than those of any of the great theologians and philosophers of the High and late Middle Ages. "In all her work she conformed to doctrine," the contemporary chronicler noted. Consequently, we cannot warn strongly enough against any attempt to take her writings and meditations out of the context of her oeuvre and isolate them in gnostic fashion, as happens time and again—in our image-hungry but image-poor times—in the New Age movement and as part of depth psychology's pursuit of self-realization.

What we find particularly fascinating in Hildegard's writings—as sensual as they are intellectually stimulating—is her religious orthodoxy, which was actually quite unusual given the large number of heresies in the history of Christian dogma. Hildegard believed in a Christianity that consisted essentially of the doctrines of Incarnation and Resurrection. In this sense, she never viewed humanity and the world, body and soul, nature and grace as isolated phenomena, but always and everywhere in the context of and in harmony with all phenomena.

Among the various disciplines, those most likely to be affected by Hildegard's movement toward modernity are the two that will likely emerge as the major disciplines of the third millennium—theology and medicine. In the case of the new medicine the effect of Hildegard's ideas will be to combine anthropologically-based thinking with ethically- and ecologically-oriented action, and in the case of the new theology it will be to create a demand for religious thinking and action that is more mystically oriented and less dogmatically rigid and morally narrow.

The fields of medicine and theology were particularly close to Hildegard's heart and constituted the core of her view of the world. They will doubtless set the tone of the new millennium.

Bibliography

ABBREVIATIONS AND SOURCES

PL   *S. Hildegardis Abbatissae Opera.* Ed. J.-P. Migne. *Patrologia Latina*, tom. 197. Parisiis 1882.

Sc   *Scivias.* In *Patrologia Latina* 197, col. 383–738.

LVM   *Liber Vitae Meritorum.* In *Analecta Sanctae Hildegardis Opera Spicilegio Solesmensi parata.* Ed. J.B. Pitra, *Analecta Sacra*, tom. 8, pp. 1–244.

LDO   *Liber Divinorum Operum.* In: *Patrologia Latina* 197, col 739–1038.

CC   *Causae et Curae.* Ed. Paul Kaiser. Lipsiae [Leipzig], 1903.

Ph   *Physica.* In: *Patrologia Latina* 197, col. 1117–1124.

V   *Vita Sanctae Hildegardis auctoribus Godefrido et Theodorico monachis.* *Patrologia Latina* 197, col. 115–130.

Bw   *Briefwechsel. Nach den ältesten Handschriften übersetzt von* [Translated from the earliest manuscripts by] *Adelgundis Führkötter.* Salzburg, 1965.

P   *Analecta Sacra*, tom. 8. Ed. J.B. Pitra. Monte Cassinense, 1882.

THE COMPLETE WORKS OF HILDEGARD IN GERMAN

Wisse die Wege. Der heiligen Hildegard von Bingen Wisse die Wege. Scivias. Ed. and transl. Maura Böckeler. 6th ed., Salzburg, 1976.

Heilkunde. Das Buch von dem Grund und Wesen und der Heilung der Krankheiten. Ed. and transl. Heinrich Schipperges. 4th ed., Salzburg, 1984.

Naturkunde. Das Buch von dem inneren Wesen der verschiedenen Naturen in der Schöpfung. Ed. and transl. Peter Riethe. Salzburg, 1959.

Welt und Mensch. Das Buch "De operatione Dei". Ed. and transl. Heinrich Schipperges. Salzburg, 1965.

Lieder. Edited from the manuscripts by Pudentiana Barth, M. Immaculata Ritscher, and Joseph Schmidt-Görg. Salzburg, 1969.

Briefwechsel. Translated from the earliest manuscripts by Adelgundis Führkötter. Salzburg, 1965.

Der Mensch in der Verantwortung. Das Buch der Lebensverdienste (Liber Vitae Meritorum). Ed. and transl. Heinrich Schipperges. Salzburg, 1972.

SECONDARY LITERATURE IN GERMAN

Albrecht, Barbara. *Gottes Werk: der Mensch*. Vallendar, 1992.

Böckeler, Maura. *Das große Zeichen. Die Frau als Symbol göttlicher Wirklichkeit*. Salzburg, 1941.

Bonn, Caecilia. *Der Mensch in der Entscheidung. Gedanken zur ganzheitlichen Schau Hildegards von Bingen*. Eltville, 1986.

———. *Mut zur Ganzheitlichkeit. Aspekte bei Hildegard von Bingen*. Eltville, 1990.

Brück, Anton Ph., ed. *Hildegard von Bingen 1179–1979. Festschrift zum 800. Todestag der Heiligen*. Mainz, 1979.

Chávez Alvarez, Fabio. *"Die brennende Vernunft". Studien zur Semantik der "rationalitas" bei Hildegard von Bingen*. Stuttgart–Bad Cannstatt, 1991.

Clarus, Ludwig. *Leben und Schriften der heilige Hildegard*. 2 vols. Regensburg, 1854.

Dronke, Peter. *Problemata Hildegardiana*. In: *Mittellateinisches Jahrbuch* 16 (1981), pp. 97–131.

Eltz, Monika zu. *Hildegard*. Freiburg, Basel, Wien, 1963.

Engels, Odilo. *Die Zeit der heilige Hildegard*. In: Anton Ph. Brück, ed., *Hildegard von Bingen 1179–1979. Festschrift*, pp. 1–29.

Führkötter, Adelgundis. *Hildegard von Bingen*. In: Hermann Hempel, Theodor Heuss, and Benno Reifenberg, eds., *Die Großen Deutschen*, vol. 5, pp. 39–47. Berlin, 1958.

Goebels, Hildegard. *Hildegard von Bingen: Mensch ihrer Zeit—Zeichen für unsere Zeit*. In: *Erbe und Auftrag* 66 (1990), pp. 209–223.

Hattemer, Margarete. *Geschichte und Erkrankungen der heiligen Hildegard von Bingen*. In: *Hippokrates* 3 (1930/31), pp. 125–149.

Herwegen, Ildefons. *Die heilige Hildegard im Lichte ihrer geschichtlichen Sendung*. In: *Der katholische Gedanke* 3 (1930), pp. 15–30.

Kerner, Charlotte. *Alle Schönheit des Himmels. Die Lebensgeschichte der Hildegard von Bingen.* Weinheim, Basel, 1993.

Klaes, Monika. *Zu Schau und Deutung des Kosmos beis Hildegard von Bingen.* In: Adelgundis Führkötter, ed., *Kosmos und Mensch aus der Sicht Hildegards von Bingen,* pp. 37–124. Mainz, 1987.

Lautenschläger, Gabriele. *Hildegard von Bingen. Die theologische Grundlegung ihrer Ethik und Spiritualität.* Stuttgart–Bad Cannstatt, 1993.

Lauter, Werner. *Hildegard-Bibliographie. Wegweiser zur Hildegard-Literatur.* 2 vols. Alzey, 1970/84.

Das Leben der heiligen Hildegard, berichtet von den Mönchen Gottfried und Theoderich. Transl. from the Latin and commentary by Adelgundis Führkötter. Salzburg, 1980.

Liebeschütz, Hans. *Das allegorische Weltbild der heiligen Hildegard von Bingen.* Leipzig, 1930.

Meier, Christel. *Die Bedeutung der Farben im Werk Hildegards von Bingen.* In: *Frühmittelalterliche Studien* 6 (1972), pp. 245–355.

Müller, Irmgard. *Krankheit und Heilmittel im Werk Hildegards von Bingen.* In: Anton Ph. Brück, ed., *Hildegard von Bingen 1179–1979. Festschrift,* pp. 311–349.

———. *Die pflanzlichen Heilmittel bei Hildegard von Bingen.* Salzburg, 1982.

Ohly, Friedrich. *Vom geistigen Sinn des Wortes im Mittelalter.* In: *Schriften zur mittelalterlichen Bedeutungsforschung,* pp. 1–31. Darmstadt, 1983.

Rozumek, Angela. *Die sittliche Weltanschauung der heiligen Hildegard von Bingen (1098–1179).* Ph.D. diss., Bonn, 1934.

Schipperges, Heinrich. *Krankheitsursache, Krankheitswesen und Heilung in der Klostermedizin, dargestellt am Welt-Bild Hildegardis von Bingen.* Med. diss., Bonn, 1951.

———. *Das Bild des Menschen bei Hildegard von Bingen. Beitrag zur philosophischen Anthropologie des 12. Jahrhunderts.* Ph.D. diss, Bonn, 1952.

———. *Hildegard von Bingen, Geheimnis der Liebe. Bilder von des Menschen leibhaftiger Not und Seligkeit.* Olten, 1957.

———. *Hildegard von Bingen, Gott ist am Werk. Die Schöpfung der Welt in Gottes Ebenbild.* Olten, 1958.

———. *Das Schöne in der Welt Hildegards von Bingen. Jahrbuch für Aesthetik und allgemeine Kunstwissenschaft* 4 (1958/59), pp. 83–139.

———. *Das Menschenbild Hildegards von Bingen. Die anthropologische Bedeutung von "Opus" in ihrem Weltbild.* Leipzig, 1962.

———. *Die Welt der Engel bei Hildegard von Bingen.* Salzburg, 1963.

———. *Die Benediktiner in der Medizin des frühen Mittelalters.* Leipzig, 1965.

———, ed. *Hildegard von Bingen. Gotteserfahrung und Weg in die Welt.* Olten, Freiburg, 1979.

———. *Mensch und Kosmos in der Medizin des hohen Mittelalters.* In: Maja Slivar, ed., *Mensch und Kosmos,* pp. 212–230. Bern, 1980.

———. *Hildegard von Bingen. Ein Zeichen für unsere Zeit.* Frankfurt am Main, 1981.

Schmelzeis, Johann Philipp. *Das Leben und Wirken der heiligen Hildegardis, nach Quellen dargestellt.* Freiburg, 1879.

Schrader, Marianna. *Heimat und Sippe der deutschen Seherin Hildegard.* Salzburg, 1941.

Schrader, Marianna/Führkötter, Adelgundis. *Die Echtheit des Schrifttums der heiligen Hildegard von Bingen. Quellenkritische Untersuchungen.* Köln [Cologne], Graz, 1956.

Sölle, Dorothee. *O Grün des Fingers Gottes. Die Meditationen der Hildegard von Bingen.* Wuppertal, 1989.

Ungrund, Magna. *Die metaphysische Anthropologie der heiligen Hildegard von Bingen.* Münster, 1938.

Wasmann, Peter. *Die heilige Hildegard als älteste deutsche Naturforscherin.* Leipzig, 1913.

Werthmann, Annelore. *Die Seherin Hildegard. Rückzug in eine großartige Welt innerer Bilder.* In: *Die Erhöhung der Frau. Psychoanalytische Untersuchungen zum Einfluß der Frau in einer sich transformierenden Gesellschaft,* pp. 145–279. Frankfurt am Main, 1993.

Widmer, Bertha. *Heilsordnung und Zeitgeschehen in der Mystik Hildegards von Bingen.* Ph.D. diss., Basel, 1955.

Zimmerman, Gerd. *Ordensleben und Lebensstandard. Die Cura corporis in den Ordensvorschriften des abendländischen Hochmittelalters.* Münster, 1973.

Secondary Literature in English

Dronke, Peter. *Women Writers of the Middle Ages.* Cambridge, 1984.

Gössmann, Elisabeth. *The Philosophical Anthropology of Hildegard of Bingen.* In: *Mystics Quarterly* 13 (1987), pp. 146–154.

Newman, Barbara. *Sister of Wisdom. St. Hildegard's Theology of the Feminine.* Berkeley, Los Angeles, London: University of California Press, 1987.

Singer, Charles. *The scientific views and visions of Saint Hildegard. Studies in the history and method of science.* Oxford, 1917.

Bibliography for Further Reading

compiled by Barbara Newman

Latin editions

Scivias, ed. Adelgundis Führkötter and Angela Carlevaris. Corpus Christianorum Continuatio Mediaevalis [CCCM] vols. 43–43a. Turnhout: Brepols, 1978.

Liber vite meritorum, ed. Angela Carlevaris, CCCM vol. 90. Turnhout: Brepols, 1995.

Liber divinorum operum, ed. Albert Derolez and Peter Dronke, CCCM. Turnhout: Brepols, forthcoming 1997.

Causae et curae, ed. Paul Kaiser. Leipzig: Teubner, 1903.

Epistolarium, ed. Lieven van Acker, CCCM vols. 91–91a. Turnhout: Brepols, 1991, 1993.

Symphonia armonie celestium revelationum (Latin and English), ed. Barbara Newman. Ithaca, N.Y.: Cornell University Press, 1988.

Vita sanctae Hildegardis, ed. Monika Klaes, CCCM vol. 126. Turnhout: Brepols, 1993.

English Translations

Hildegard of Bingen: Mystical Writings, ed. Fiona Bowie and Oliver Davies, transl. Robert Carver. New York: Crossroad, 1990.

Letters of Hildegard of Bingen, Vol. 1, transl. Joseph Baird and Radd Ehrman. Oxford University Press, 1994. Vol. 2 forthcoming, 1997.

Scivias, transl. Columba Hart and Jane Bishop, in: Classics of Western Spirituality series. Mahwah, N.J.: Paulist Press, 1990.

Secrets of God: Writings of Hildegard of Bingen, transl. Sabina Flanagan. Boston: Shambhala, 1996.

Symphonia, transl. Barbara Newman. Ithaca: Cornell, 1988.

Studies

Dronke, Peter. *Women Writers of the Middle Ages: A Critical Study of Texts from Perpetua to Marguerite Porete*. Cambridge University Press, 1984.

Flanagan, Sabina. *Hildegard of Bingen, 1098–1179: A Visionary Life*. London: Routledge, 1989.

Newman, Barbara. *Sister of Wisdom: St. Hildegard's Theology of the Feminine*. Berkeley: University of California Press, 1987.

Index